1870

1970s

1910

MANICKE

The Story of
AMERICAN HUNTING
and FIREARMS

The Story of American Hunting and Firearms

The Story of AMERICAN

Updated and Revised

with a preface by Jim Carmichel,
Shooting Editor, *Outdoor Life*

with paintings by RALPH CROSBY SMITH

drawings by Nicholas Eggenhofer *and* Ray Pioch

HUNTING and FIREARMS

From OUTDOOR LIFE

OUTDOOR LIFE

Sunrise Books / E. P. Dutton & Company, Inc.

New York

CONTENTS

Preface to the revised and updated edition

By Jim Carmichel, Shooting Editor, *Outdoor Life*

On the 200th birthday of the United States all Americans would do well to reflect on our heritage of great firearms and the men who used them. No history of the nation's development could be complete without a detailed examination of American guns and, in fact, as readers of this book will soon discover, the history of American firearms is itself a rich chronicle of American achievement.

Such legendary figures as Daniel Boone, Andrew Jackson, Davy Crockett, Jim Bridger, Wild Bill Hickok, Theodore Roosevelt, and Sergeant Alvin York, to name a few, might never have strode into the annals of immortality had it not been for their ability to use a firearm. Had it not been for the rifle over the colonial mantel and a willingness to use it in the cause of freedom, there would be no Bicentennial —no America.

Along the way our language has become rich with the idioms of the gun; going off half cocked, a flash in the pan, ramrod straight, and dozens of others are common phrases everyone uses without realizing their shooting origin.

Also, too few of us are aware that the greatest sports heroes of the last century were competitive marksmen and that the rifle tournaments held against other nations were banner headline news as well as the most avidly attended sporting events of the day.

This is the story of American hunting and firearms, from the early settlers who made their way into the "dark and bloody ground of Kentucky"—the region which gave its name to the graceful long rifles they carried—to the modern sportsman who has mastered the science of giving back to nature what he takes from it.

ILLUSTRATIONS

ILLUSTRATIONS (Continued)

CHAPTER 1

The First American Hunters

The first white colonists, huddled in their tiny coastal settlements on the edge of the New World, looked upon the great forest that stretched out into a green unknown as an awesome and forbidding wilderness. Yet that wilderness, for at least ten thousand years, had been the home of the American Indian. The story of hunting in America, then, begins with the Indian, his ingenious weapons and techniques, his methods of conservation, and the influence of his religious beliefs.

The American Indian was an expert hunter and fisherman—he had to be if he wanted to live. Although he enjoyed the hunt as a sportsman and made it an important part of his religious life, he felt an urgent necessity behind his search for game. For most Indian tribes, the bulk of essential food came from the wild creatures of the forests, plains, and waters.

The only domesticated animals the Indian had before the wild horses of the Spaniards spread over the plains were dogs. He had no cattle, pigs, sheep, or fowl. The dogs were used in hunting and as beasts of burden, pulling sledges or *travois*, not as food. When the Indian needed meat he had to hunt for it or fish it from the rivers and lakes.

Wild game gave him more than food. Animal skins were used for clothing, shelters, and bowstrings; antlers were cut into arrow tips; and bones became knives, awls, combs, fishhooks, needles, arrow and spear points, rubbing tools, scrapers, and spoons.

It is little wonder that the American Indian became perhaps the most accomplished outdoorsman the world has known, since wild animals supplied so many necessities of life. He used every method of catching game— traps, stalking, stillhunting, and mass drives involving a whole family or tribe. He devised every possible weapon or tool for hunting and fishing that could be made by stone-age man —spears, clubs, throwing sticks, blowguns, bows and arrows, traps, nets, poisons, harpoons. The weapons he used, the methods he followed depended upon the game available and the environment in which he lived. And he recognized that this game represented his greatest natural resource, and that it must be permitted to propagate and replenish itself.

We need to remind ourselves that the general false impression of the Indians as one close-knit, uniform people originally derives from Columbus' mistake in believing he had reached the fabled Indies and his application of one name to what were really many decidedly contrasting groups. The approximately one million Indians that lived north of the Rio Grande and south of the Arctic Circle at the time of America's discovery were divided into about four hundred different tribes and subtribes. These tribes varied enormously in physical traits, in their sometimes completely different languages and in their pattern of communal life, wherein hunting played a significant role.

The early white explorers encountered the forest Indians of the Eastern section of the country, and frontiersmen pushing westward many decades later became familiar with the Indians of the Plains. But there were many other groups, such as the Southeastern Indians, the Mound Builders and their successors, who were largely agricultural, and the tribes of the Southwest such as the Pueblo, Hopi, and Navaho, who were almost entirely agricultural because there was little game in their territory. Then there were the Indians of the Northwest, among them the Coeur d'Alene, Wenatchee, and Chehalis, whose lives revolved around the two most plentiful natural resources in their region, game and wood, those near the coast depending heavily on salmon and sea mammals.

No matter what the tribe or the region in which it lived, every able-bodied man was expected to be a proficient hunter, angler, and warrior. And he began to learn these skills early in life. Boys were taught to make their own small bows and arrows, with which they had shooting contests—a bear's paw hanging from a branch was a common target. Or one of a group of boys would shoot his arrow into an open field; the others then shot, each trying to make his arrow land across the first. In some tribes boys made hoops of vines, with smaller vines dividing the circle into sections of different sizes. Then they shot at the hoop as it rolled, each boy trying to send his arrow through the smallest section of the moving target. Such games were excellent training for hunting fast-running deer or antelope.

The few unfortunates who had some physical defect or who were *berdaches*—female souls in men's bodies—were scorned or pitied. They took up the life and tasks of women, sometimes even wearing women's clothing. They cooked the food, "kept house," tanned skins, made clothes and pots, and tended the gardens of maize, squash, pumpkins, beans, and tobacco.

The Indian hunter and warrior prided himself on his courage and his stamina. He could not cry out, no matter what pain he suffered. He could not complain or even show fatigue, no matter how long it took to bag his game. An Indian could run steadily for ten to twelve hours without eating, and sometimes this was necessary. When game was scarce he might have to pursue his quarry for three or four days without food; but he could not come back without having made some kind of kill.

For both hunting and war, the Indian had to train himself from boyhood in tracking and stalking. As modern hunters know, stalking is an art requiring an abundance of patience and stealth, intimate knowledge of the woods and the habits of the creatures he is hunting. And even with these skills highly developed, he is often outsmarted by a wary and keenly sensitive beast. Since his life depended on the game he caught, the Indian had to develop the art of stalking to a high degree of perfection. He learned to observe, as he moved swiftly through the forest, the broken twigs, the crushed moss, the disturbed leaves, the scattered pebbles which told him that an enemy or an animal had passed that way. His silence in the forest and his near-invisibility have become part of the American legend. In his moccasined feet and wearing only a loin cloth or, in winter, leggings and a fur robe, he could move like a ghost along a game trail, with his spear or bow ready for immediate action. He could freeze into instant immobility and remain motionless for long periods, during which it took a keen eye to see him. He bathed thoroughly before hunting so that his human scent would not be carried to the game; he sometimes rubbed his body with leaves or, as among the Abenaki of the Northeast, with sweet-smelling ferns commonly found in their forests.

Many tribes stalked their prey in disguise. Some Western Indians covered themselves with animal skins, dropped down on all fours, and crept close to herds of antelope or even grazing buffaloes. When they were within range they shot their arrows—a highly dangerous maneuver especially when hunting buffaloes. If the braves' arrows merely wounded the buffalo, the enraged animal was a formidable opponent; he died slowly and, until he dropped, was fast on his feet and determined to gore or trample into the dust the creature that had sent the sharp shafts into his body.

Among Eastern tribes, deer were the usual prey of those who stalked in disguise. The Pamunkey Indians of eastern Virginia, leading tribe of the Powhatan Confederacy, were particularly skilled in this method of hunting. Each member of a stalking party covered himself with a deerskin, in which eyeholes had been cut. Clutching his bow and arrows and crouching so low that he frequently moved on hands and knees, with the skin's legs dangling to the ground and the antlers tossing overhead, he crept toward his deer. At close range, and with his ability to shoot arrows so rapidly that several might be in the air at once, the Indian might bring down several deer before they all darted away.

Some Indians engaged in what might be called underwater stalking. They hid from enemies in water, breathing through hollow reeds, or floated under logs to a strategic point of attack on an enemy village. The same methods were occasionally used in hunting. A California Indian, after locating a flock of ducks feeding on a stream, would let some hollow gourds float down among them, until the birds no longer paid any attention to them. Then, putting his head inside a large gourd with peepholes, he would float down among the ducks. When he was near enough, he would grab an unsuspecting duck by the legs and pull it under the water, sometimes so quickly that the other ducks were not even disturbed. If he was particularly adept at this, he might snare several ducks for himself before the others took alarm and flew away.

Indians made and used a great variety of traps to catch game and birds. The noose, made of vines, was a common catching device along a trail. The Iroquois, the Menomini, and many other tribes fastened a noose to a sapling, which was bent over and "cocked" delicately under a branch of another tree. As the animal walked into the noose and pulled it forward, the bent sapling slid from beneath the branch and snapped into the air, hanging the quarry. Some noose traps were contrived so that the animal stepped into the noose, which then suspended it by the legs until the hunter came. In some cases the Indians put a baited noose on the game trail and waited patiently until some animal came along and stepped into it, and then the hunter pulled the noose tight.

In regions where bear and other large fur-bearing animals lived, the deadfall was often used. Heavy logs were held up by a carefully balanced stick to which bait, or a separate bait stick, was attached. The smallest tug on the bait dislodged the upright and the logs crashed down, pinning the animal to the earth. Other good-sized animals were caught

The simple noose trap of the Iroquois consisted of a piece of bark with a hole in it and a noose of bark twine. When a bird pecked at the bait in the hole, the twine slipped over his neck, caught in his feathers, and held him fast.

Many Eastern Indians bagged small game with the blowgun, shooting small, sharp darts in complete silence.

in pits with inward-sloping sides that prevented the trapped animal from climbing or jumping out. The hole was covered with light branches and leaves, with bait placed in the middle. In some instances the covering was much stronger and could bear the weight of the animal that stepped on it to take the bait. The Indian hunter waited in the pit below, and speared his quarry as it stood above him.

Indians trapped smaller game, too. The Penobscot Indians, for example, caught mink and sable by using a still reliable method—let them in but don't let them out. One of these traps was merely a small baited hole cut in the side of a tree not too far above the ground. The trap maker then drove two sharp sticks through the bark and up through the bottom of the hole so they angled toward each other and at the same time slanted toward the rear. The animal could squeeze its head past them to get the bait, but couldn't pull its head out again.

A similar method was used by the Iroquois, among others, to catch birds. The trap was a piece of elm bark about four inches wide and eight inches long, near one end of which a hole or eye was cut. A noose of bark twine was looped around the hole, with the free end fastened at the other end of the bark. The Indian dropped a little corn in the eye and waited for a hungry bird to come along. When the bird pecked the corn, the noose caught in the ruffled feathers of its neck and tightened as it tried to fly away.

In the making and setting of all traps the Indians were careful to remove, so far as they could, all traces of man. The dirt from pit traps was carried far away. Anything that the hands had touched was either washed or smoked to remove the warning scent of the human enemy.

Pamunkey braves, as well as the hunters of other Eastern tribes, bagged much of their small game and many birds with blowguns— a quiet weapon that in time spread to the Cherokee and even into some of the other Iroquois tribes. Most blowguns were about ten feet long, made of cane or elder, and used light, sharp darts—rarely poisoned, as were many blowgun darts among the Central and South American Indians. A high degree of proficiency could be obtained with the blowgun, which had the advantage of complete silence; not even the twang of a bowstring could alert the game to the source of the attack.

The bow and arrow, of course, was the most common weapon among all Indians of

North America. The natives of the Southwest originally used the *atlatl,* or throwing stick, but soon adopted the bow and arrow from neighboring tribes who had proved the effectiveness of the weapon even where game was scarce.

Until the coming of the horse to the Plains and the Southwest—around the middle of the sixteenth century—most Indian bows were long. The short bow came in with the horse, because it was easily handled by a mounted hunter. Most bows were made of carefully selected woods—preferably hickory, white oak, or hemlock. The Indian cut from a felled tree a block of wood that had the necessary strength and grain—no small task with his primitive tools—and carried it home, where he carved it slowly with a bone knife into the final curved form he wished it to have. He rubbed it with bear grease and set it aside for seasoning. To keep the bow from cracking, he sized it at regular intervals with deer brains. The earlier Menomini made his bow perfectly straight, but he had to be careful not to draw the string back too far for fear the bow might crack or the arrow might be erratic in its flight; as the years passed he learned, from nearby tribes, to give the weapon its graceful and efficient curve.

The Indian bowstring was made of twisted rawhide. Big-game arrows, of straight-grained wood, were usually tipped with finely-barbed stone, inserted in a circular hole burned or bored in the end of the shaft. When the arrow struck an animal the shaft usually fell to the ground, while the barb dug in more deeply with each movement of the wounded animal. But since stone points often stopped upon hitting bone, the Menomini frequently used tips made of deer antlers, which were tougher and less brittle and penetrated deeply.

Many Indians discarded arrowheads when hunting small game and relied upon the missile customarily used in target practice—an all-wood arrow with a blunt tip, capable of striking a stunning, if not killing, blow upon a small animal or bird. Some Indians also changed the stone tip for battling enemy tribes, when they might use an arrowhead made from a turtle claw, stuck firmly in place with sturgeon glue—a double dose of potent magic which presumably added to the effectiveness of the weapon.

In any event, arrows were precious possessions, difficult to make. No Indian wasted arrows, no matter how many he had. On his hunts he usually carried a stone club which was made of a flat stone so that it would be comfortable when tucked in his belt. If he wounded a deer, he would follow it until it went down, then administer the *coup de grâce* with the stone club.

The club was the preferred weapon in dealing with bears, too. The truly great hunter, stalking a bear until it turned to confront him, approached the great beast and hit it over the head with his club. Perhaps one practical reason for this was that the bear, so heavily protected by fur, tough skin, and a layer of fat, was more often wounded by arrows than killed outright. And a wounded bear was an even more dangerous adversary than a wounded bison. But there were other elements in the Indian's thinking. To him a bear was, of all wild creatures, most like a man—near in size and similar in his occasional walking on two legs. The Indian felt that he must approach the bear on an equal footing, except for the stone club, which was offset by the bear's superior size and strength.

In many tribes the hunter apologized to the bear before killing it; most Indians believed that animals could understand their words, their thoughts, even their songs. The bear, in the Indian's opinion, was a coward. The Indian was not a coward. At the first blow of the club, many Indians claimed, the bear crumpled to the ground and "cried." At this point the Indian would tell the bear he was sorry, but that he had to kill him for meat and fat and fur. If the bear was brave rather than cowardly, the Indian knew that the bear would use his great strength to kill him.

Although the white settlers who later battled the grizzly would not have shared the opinion, most Indians were so convinced of the bear's basic cowardice that the Menomini, for example, would enter a bear's cave armed only with a long spear and take him on in a showdown battle on his own ground. Since the Menomini believed themselves to be descended from the Great Underground Bear, a particularly strong apology, with a somewhat religious flavor, was necessary before the kill. For meat and fur, the Indian had to kill the beast that was to him almost a brother.

During the months when bears prowled through the woods looking for food, they were often hunted with the bow and arrow plus the stone club, as were deer and other creatures. For much of his hunting the Indian went out alone. He might stillhunt, stationing himself near some animal path or at a watering place, and remain immobile until his quarry came along. In the case of the big, lumbering bear, he might pursue the beast until it dropped from exhaustion, after which he could finish it off with his club.

During the winter months many of the Northern Indian hunters went out on snowshoes to hunt moose. The Penobscot Indians, living in what is now Maine, were particularly skillful in using the wide, webbed footgear. Many a Penobscot brave set out alone on a winter day armed with bow and arrow and a determination to get his moose. When he sighted his game, frequently in its winter yard, he wounded it with an arrow—the beast was so big and tough that one arrow could do little more—and then trailed it across the snow, getting in another shot whenever he could. He tried to drive the animal toward drifts of deep snow, where the moose was likely to flounder because of its great weight and sharp hoofs. The Indian, with his snowshoes, could travel swiftly and catch up to his prey, where a final shaft would finish it off.

Then the big problem, of course, was to get the beast home. In winter, the task was sometimes made easier because the hunter could fashion a sledge of bark and pull his undressed moose or deer back to his village. At other times the Indian skinned his game on the spot, built a fire, and cured or dried the slabs of meat, which could be packed in bark barrels or the skins and carried on his back.

Hunting in canoe or dugout, either alone or with one or two companions, often made the transportation problem simpler. This method was commonly used by Indians in the East. The braves sometimes hunted deer at night using jacklights to attract them. They made false salt licks, if they had the material, and waved salty branches in the air to bring the game to them. Sometimes they waited in their canoes where deer, caribou, bears, and antelope were known to swim; or companions would force the animals into the water when they came to drink. But there were always dangers in hunting from a canoe; a wounded beast often tried to clamber into the boat.

The Coeur d'Alene Indian who ranged just south of the Canadian border in the Northwest, was clever at hunting animals by forcing them into the water, where they moved so slowly that they were more easily killed with spears or arrows. But the Coeur d'Alene also used a hooked stick, which he thrust into a swimming deer's antlers, after which he forced the animal's head under water until it drowned. Even without weapons of any kind the Coeur d'Alene brave did not hesitate to tackle a swimming deer, elk, or moose and drown it.

Far to the south, in what is today Florida, resourceful Indians contrived an unusual way to kill the alligators that infested the region. The first step was to build an enclosed watchtower with several peepholes. One Indian stood guard in this structure, waiting for an alligator to climb from the water onto dry land. Then he signaled the hunters concealed on the shore, who rushed up carrying a pointed ten-foot pole as if it were a battering ram.

They thrust the pole down the reptile's throat and the rough bark prevented it from slipping out. Then they flopped the 'gator over on its back and clubbed it to death or killed it with arrows.

In most regions fishing supplemented hunting as a source of food, and in some sections the bulk of the food supply came from the water. Indians used fishhooks made of bone, but they were also good at catching a large number of fish at one time by damming a stream and using big nets made of vines, or bark cord, or by spreading poison herbs over the water. They also spearfished, and devised many different kinds of nets and traps.

Perhaps the most expert fishermen were the tribes of the far Northwest, where agriculture was almost unknown and the game not too plentiful. The rivers, straits, and bays, and the sea itself, abounded in fish, however. During the salmon runs Indians speared them by the hundreds, and a family had not only plenty of fresh fish for a while but as much as a ton of dried salmon stored away. During herring runs thousands of fish were taken in nets, but some Indians used a most unusual method of catching them. Two men set out in a dugout canoe and paddled to the center of the mass of swimming herring. One of the paddles was made with a series of sharp spikes along one edge. As this paddler pushed through the thick mass of herring, he managed to snag one or more on the spikes. With a flip, he tossed the fish into the boat, and then took another productive stroke.

The Nootka Indians of the far Northwest built magnificent dugouts, some of which were as much as fifty feet long. In these they hunted for sea lions, porpoises, and even whales. But whale-fishing was so hazardous that it was usually preceded by elaborate rituals of a religious nature. Similar rites were common among most Indian tribes before any hunt involving a great many braves. A mass hunt was both a great social and a significant religious event in many groups. There was often solemn dancing, sometimes fasting by the

The Penobscot brave used wide, webbed snowshoes to follow a moose through deep snow, shooting his arrows into the heavy animal as it floundered in the snow.

leaders of the hunt, who also prepared special and sacred batons of office. Some tribes insisted that even the arrows used on a hunt had to be treated to the medicine man's specifications. In most Northern tribes a sacred tobacco was smoked in a long-stemmed pipe, or calumet, after the route of the hunt had been determined or the quarry had been sighted. In all cases there were customs that had to be followed rigidly and innumerable taboos to be observed. The discipline on a tribal hunt was strict.

The nature of a mass drive or tribal hunt depended upon the game and the terrain. Most deer drives involved some kind of huge corral which enabled the hunters to force the deer unsuspectingly down a gradually narrowing passageway, where other hunters awaited them. The Menomini prepared for the hunt by felling many trees to form a giant V, which ran for several miles through the woods. The trees were dropped so that the trunks remained attached to the stumps but lay close to the ground, all extending in the same direction.

When the drive began, a band of hunters concealed themselves at the apex of the V.

Other hunters—and sometimes their women and children—gathered at the wide end of the V and, walking slowly and noisily forward, moved toward the bottleneck. The deer fled before them, but the drive had to be well paced. If the hunters moved too fast, the deer became panicky and leaped over the fallen logs and out of the V. But when the hunters proceeded cautiously, the deer followed the line of least resistance inside the barricade and finally found themselves trapped.

The Iroquois usually made their barricades with a brush fence two or three miles long, and they started the drive by setting fire to the woods back of the wide end of the corral. Parties of braves patrolled the sides of the V to prevent most deer from leaping over it, so they were eventually driven to the apex, where other hunters shot them.

Some Western Indians did not use the long corral, however, but took advantage of the deer's fear of the smell of scorched buffalo hides. The day before such a drive, each member of the hunting party brought to the chief a piece of buffalo hide and a sharp stick on which to carry it. The chief scorched the skins and, the next morning, took them to a suitable spot

Armed only with a stone-tipped, wooden spear, the Menomini brave wasn't afraid to enter a dark cave to meet a bear on his own ground.

about five miles to the windward of the hunters' starting point. There he stuck each stick with its hide into the earth, in a line parallel to the approaching braves before whom the deer were retreating. The chief, well hidden from the deer, watched them progress toward him. As they scented the scorched skins and turned to run away from them, he gave a signal and advanced. The hunters lay down while the chief moved ahead, yelling and waving his arms. The frightened deer fled even more swiftly from this new danger, straight toward the hidden hunters, who raised to their knees and killed them as they came within range.

In some deer drives the Indian hunters were fortunate enough to have within their territory a natural corral, such as a narrow gorge, into which the deer could be driven. In other areas there were cliffs, with a projecting ledge a few feet below the brink; in such places, a few braves wearing deerskins stood on the edge of the cliff as other hunters drove the deer toward them. The fleeing deer, seeing what they thought were others of their kind in a safe place, raced for the cliff. The disguised hunters leaped to the ledge below and the main body charged against the deer, many of which plunged over the cliff to their death below. The same method was used, on occasion, on buffalo hunts.

The use of a natural trap in a mass drive was skillfully developed against one of the most elusive of all game animals, the mountain goat. As today's hunters know, these creatures are not often caught in a telescopic sight, and even the strongest climber and stalker would be lost without a high-powered rifle. But the Indians of the Northwest mountain regions hunted the mountain goat with spears! To succeed, they needed a hardy and experienced hunting party, each member of which knew the terrain well; they needed a natural gorge of some kind, and the help of the proper religious spirits.

With a few hunters, armed with spears, ready at the narrow pass or gorge, the main body, several miles back, made its way slowly —and not too quietly—down from the ridges into the narrowing valley. The mountain goats, not too alarmed at these intruders who never came too close for comfort, moved away from them, down the slopes and into the gorge. In time the goats found themselves trapped, easy prey for the hunters and their spears.

By far the largest of all mass hunts were those for buffalo. Both before and after the coming of the horse they were community enterprises, involving men, women, children, and dogs. Entire villages—or even several villages—picked up and moved when the scouts reported the sighting of big herds. Why did all the members of a tribe move to the scene of the buffalo hunt, rather than just the hunters? Because there was so much work to be done. This was the one big chance to obtain a year's supply of the essentials of life, and the tribe hoped to make a big killing. Most of the meat had to be "jerked"—cut in thin strips and sun-dried. The hides had to be scraped and tanned, a task usually handled by the women. There was plenty of work for everyone.

The buffalo hunts were usually annual affairs, taking place when the huge migrating herds came near a particular tribe's territory. As that time approached, scouts were sent out to search for the herds, and many pre-hunt rituals were engaged in—to purify the bodies of all hunters and to invoke the aid of whatever spirits the tribe believed in. The rituals and the spirits varied, for there were many different and unrelated tribes on the Great Plains where the buffalo roamed. However, their customs, houses, and social organizations were remarkably similar, since they were determined by the environment in which they lived and by their dependence upon the buffalo as their chief source of food, clothing, tools, and even housing.

Before the horse, when dogs were the only beasts of burden used on the buffalo hunt, the tepee poles had to be short—they were used as the framework of the *travois*—loads had to be kept to an austere minimum, and distances traveled had to be limited. After the Indians began to catch and tame the horses, strayed or stolen from Spaniards to the south, the annual buffalo hunt was an even bigger project. Horses could carry far heavier burdens, and tribes could travel greater distances to find the big herds. Hunters on horseback could range over wider territory and pursue fleeing herds until hundreds of the big creatures were killed. As a result many of the tribes on the edges of the Great Plains abandoned farming as a major enterprise and took up buffalo hunting, for there seemed to be an unlimited supply of the animals.

As practiced by the Indians, buffalo hunting was a dangerous sport. Armed with spears or short bows and arrows, some hunters dashed into the center of the herd on their small, swift horses, while others ranged along the sides to keep the beasts in a compact mass. Still others would turn back the charge of a stampeding herd, to keep it from getting out of the range of the main body of hunters. If a brave's horse were gored in the midst of the herd, the hunter might leap on the back of one of the buffaloes until he found himself in a clear space from which he had a chance to escape. After a successful hunt a tribe might find itself with more carcasses than it could handle, in which case there was considerable waste.

Waste of game of any kind was almost unheard of among Indians, however, and oc-curred occasionally in the case of the buffalo only because of the nature of the hunt, for each brave shot down as many of the beasts as he could when the herd was attacked. In the main, Indians killed game only according to their needs, and they were always aware of the necessity of conserving the game in their territories. The Wyandot, for example, spared all female game at certain seasons. Some Iroquois tribes forbade the killing of female bears at any time. The Penobscot never took breeding beavers.

Most families among the Algonquin tribes had definite boundaries to their hunting grounds, and kept careful count of the game population within their territories. When necessary, closed seasons were enforced for species that seemed to be diminishing in number. Menomini tribal laws prohibited the wanton slaying of any wildlife, and this was accepted as a basic principle by all American Indians. They tried to teach this to the white settlers but, as subsequent events proved, had little success. It was many decades before the European immigrants to the teeming North American wilderness learned that wildlife is not inexhaustible and that measures must be taken to preserve it.

The Indian was a conservationist because he had to maintain the basic necessities of life. He was also a remarkable hunter and sportsman, one whom all modern hunters can respect for his great courage and skill with the most primitive of weapons.

CHAPTER 2

The First Firearms in America

The first explorers in North America came with firearms that terrified the Indians—and killed many of them. But without the help and friendship of those Indians—given freely at first, later erratically —many white men would have starved to death. For the harquebus, and the musket that succeeded it as the most common weapon of the Europeans, were no match for the bow and arrow and the Indians' skill in hunting game, even when game was as plentiful as the explorers and early settlers found it in the New World.

They discovered a wilderness teeming with wild birds and animals in unbelievable numbers. Animals that they had known in the Old World and some that they had never seen before were so abundant that they were sometimes a nuisance. In Florida alone, according to a Spaniard who came with the expedition of Hernando de Soto, discoverer of the Mississippi River, they found lions, bears, wolves, deer, cats, rabbits, and dogs they called "jackals," as well as partridges, cranes, ducks, pigeons, thrushes, sparrows, blackbirds, hawks, goshawks, and falcons.

Another Spaniard, writing from northern Florida in June, 1528, and very interested in the strange wildlife about him, made the first known reference to the possum when he reported seeing "an animal with a pocket on its belly in which it carries its young until they know how to seek food." A delighted Englishman told of finding on the Virginia coast twenty-eight species of animals and eighty-six different birds. In time the explorers learned that the vast continent—whose extent they did not even suspect—had buffaloes, elk, deer, bighorns, antelope, moose, wolves, foxes, beavers, otters, bears, badgers, skunks, porcupines, muskrats, and panthers, among others. It was truly a hunter's paradise.

But the first Europeans to settle in what is now the United States were poorly equipped for the gigantic task of taming a wilderness. The first English colony, established on Roanoke Island off the coast of North Carolina in 1585, was completely wiped out. The next, started at Jamestown, Virginia, in 1607, barely survived after years of trouble and suffering, and would have been given up if supplies and provisions had not been brought from England. Those who survived were driven to eating their own precious horses, their boots, and even some of their comrades who had died. The Pilgrims who landed at Plymouth, Massachusetts, in 1620 fared little better during their first bitter winter, although the help of the Indians enabled them to avoid cannibalism.

There was one simple explanation for starvation in the midst of such bounteous game: The first white man on the continent had no dependable and accurate weapon for killing the game he hunted. The Spaniards were not primarily interested in hunting game, nor did they often find it necessary, for they made their greatest progress in areas where the Indians had highly developed civilizations, as in Mexico. Here they merely conquered and enslaved the Indians and made *them* produce the necessary food. It is significant that many decades passed before the Spaniards made any considerable headway in less civilized areas, as in Florida and the southwestern part of what is now the United States. They were interested primarily in gold and silver, in mass conversions of the Indians, and using the labor of those Indians to supply their wants.

The Spaniards came with two weapons which made their conquests of the Indians possible—the horse and the harquebus. The horse had never been seen by the Indians, and to them a beast carrying a man at incredible speed and obeying his commands was supernatural. When the man also controlled the thunder and lightning, through his harquebus, he was unconquerable. The noise, the smoke, the fire all made a great impression, but in addition the harquebus left a good number of any massed group lying dead on the ground.

As a hunting weapon, however, it was not nearly as efficient as the bow and arrow. And

The Indians respected and feared the guns of the early explorers. Even friendly redskins fled in panic when a Spaniard fired his matchlock.

in all probability it was worse as a weapon of war, except for the terror inspired by its noise and the early belief—even among many Europeans—that bullet wounds were poisonous and incurable.

But there is an interesting question here. If the early firearms were so inefficient and inaccurate, how did they manage to supplant the longbow and the crossbow, which had reached a high stage of development and had many thousands of highly skilled users? The answer may be found in a brief review of the development of firearms.

Gunpowder had been invented several centuries before it was applied to arms. We know that in Europe its first use in a weapon shooting missiles came in the thirteenth or fourteenth century. The English had cannon at the battle of Crécy in 1346, although the archers with their longbows really won that fight. Within fifty years of the introduction of the cannon, men were experimenting with guns that could be carried.

The first "hand gonne" was just a heavy iron or brass tube mounted on a straight stock which could be held against the chest or under the armpit. The whole thing was about two and half to three feet long. A good charge of powder was poured down the tube, followed by a not-too-symmetrical ball weighing about an ounce. Fire at the touchhole just above the powder ignited the powder and shot out the bullet, which might hit a good-sized target if it was only about fifty yards away and if the gunner was lucky.

A heavier type of handgun, or hand cannon, sometimes called the culverin, required a crew of two men, as well as a forked rest on which the barrel of the weapon could be supported. The first man put the butt of the weapon against his chest and aimed; the second steadied the rest and applied the spark to the touchhole. He also carried a pouch of bullets and a flask of powder, and helped to load and carry the unwieldy gun. Most hand

cannons weighed from twelve to twenty pounds; the bullets, weighing one and a half to two ounces, could penetrate any but the thickest armor at close to a hundred yards. This made it at least the equal of the crossbow, a slow-firing weapon because of the necessity of winding up a windlass to pull back the steel string for each shot. Since crossbows had been the standard weapons on the European continent, the handgun began to gain acceptance there as a weapon of war. But in England, where the standard weapon was the longbow, firearms were a long time in gaining recognition. An archer could shoot twenty shafts while two men were reloading a culverin, and his range and accuracy were superior. But there was little effort in warfare at sharpshooting by either archers or gunners. The preferred technique was to send a hail of arrows or bullets against a massed enemy force.

The most serious drawback of early firearms was the need of some kind of fire or spark to ignite the powder. Sometimes a red-hot metal rod was used, but that restricted the gunner to the vicinity of a fire in which the rods could be heated. Sometimes hot coals were carried in a tinderbox, but they didn't last long. Such handicaps limited the use of handguns until the development of the "match," a long cord of hemp or flax or cotton that had been saturated in saltpeter or the lees of wine. This burned without a flame, much like the piece of "punk" with which modern youngsters light firecrackers. Usually both ends of the match were ignited, so that if one end went out, it could be relighted from the other end. But in rainy weather, of course, both ends were likely to go out.

This method of ignition was improved when the match became a part of the gun itself by being fixed in a metal serpentine (so called because of its S shape and later actually decorated to represent a serpent). This mechanism came to be known as the "matchlock." The serpentine, a kind of forerunner of the hammer, was pulled down by hand, but in time it was actuated by a lever which in turn was attached to the original form of trigger—first called the tricker, from the Dutch word for "pull." The serpentine was fixed to the side of the barrel so that its upper portion, which held the glowing match end, would swing down into the flashpan when the lower portion was pulled toward the gunner with his trigger finger. The trigger later was arranged to move the hinged cover of the flashpan as the serpentine descended. The rest of the match was looped around the barrel of the gun. As the match burned down, of course, the gunner had to loosen the setscrew that held it in the serpentine and pull the burning cord forward, then tighten the screw again. The mechanism was further refined to embody a spring element. When compressed, the spring locked the serpentine in a ready position; when released, the spring drove the holder with its lighted match into the flashpan. The matchlock with these devices was a revolutionary development because it enabled the gunner to use both hands for holding and aiming the gun, and eliminated the need for an assistant.

As the matchlock was being developed and used on the early handguns, many improvements were being made in the barrels and stocks of guns. The touchhole was removed from the top to the side of the barrel, and a small pan was placed beside it to hold the fine priming powder. Then a cover was put on the pan to keep out the rain. Gunsmiths of several European countries began to improve the shape of the stock. The weapon that evolved was the harquebus. The harquebus, first brought to America by the Spanish, incorporated the matchlock mechanism into a stock which was curved and the butt widened so that it could be fired from the shoulder. Thus shooting and aiming was more comfortable, and the accuracy was improved because both front and rear sights could be added. Although fifty yards was still about the limit for a fairly sure shot, the bullet had enough velocity and punch to kill at a hundred yards or more.

The first of the harquebuses were short, being only about three and a half feet over-all, using bullets weighing twenty to thirty to the pound. By the time the Spaniards came to the New World, the harquebus had grown longer, most of them being about four feet over-all. The bore was around three-quarters of an inch, roughly .75-caliber or 12 gauge. It was an effective weapon against a massed

A relatively advanced matchlock mechanism connected a trigger to the serpentine with an internal spring action. The cord match was held in the head of the serpentine, which was spring-locked in a "cocked" position (dotted line). When the trigger was pulled, the head of the serpentine swung down, pressing the lighted end of the match into the flashpan, igniting the priming powder.

enemy, and it frightened even friendly Indians, who would run for cover when one was fired. But it did not take them long to get over their fear and covet the weapons for themselves.

Since it was for some time the best weapon available, men did try to hunt with the harquebus. But picture yourself as one of the early Spaniards or Frenchmen or Englishmen exploring the new continent in the first half of the sixteenth century. You have some time on your hands, and the country around you abounds in game of all kinds, so you decide to go hunting with your harquebus. If you have been hunting before, you know that there is little chance of bagging anything unless you happen to come upon a flock of sitting birds or a herd of grazing deer which do not sense your approach despite the smell broadcast by your burning match. If you are unusually lucky, you may be able to tree a bear or drive some other beast to bay. You might arrange with some friends or friendly Indians to circle about and drive some game past an ambush— but they would have to drive the animals very slowly. Or you can pick a likely spot and hope a slow-moving target will lumber past.

Let us assume that a deer *does* walk past. You fire and miss, because the deer does not move slowly enough. Then what must you do? You must reload your weapon, of course. First you loosen the setscrew in the serpentine and remove the match from it, because it is too dangerous to have the burning match near powder as you are loading. Then you put the butt of your harquebus on the ground and from one flask pour the proper charge of powder into the barrel. From a pouch you take a bullet and ram it down into the barrel. Then from a second flask you measure out the proper amount of fine priming powder into the flashpan, covering it carefully afterward and making certain that no powder is on the cover.

Finally you replace the glowing match in the serpentine, fix it in place with the setscrew —and wait for another deer to amble past. But as you wait you find that the match gradually burns down to the serpentine, and you know that if it burns down to the metal it will go out. So you loosen the setscrew, pull the match forward a quarter of an inch, and tighten the setscrew. Then you wait. Meanwhile the other end of your match has gone out because it lay

This single-shot, smoothbore matchlock was made in Germany about 1660. The stock was designed to be held against the leg or under the arm of the shooter. Gun courtesy of Robert Abels, New York.

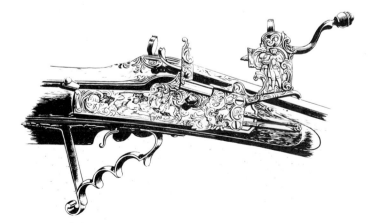

on the damp ground while you were busy with your other preparations. As you wait, you regularly adjust the match.

But you are patient and lucky. Another deer finally comes along, moving very slowly. You aim carefully, and you know that you have him. You pull the trigger—and nothing happens. The gun does not fire. Why? Who knows? Perhaps the priming powder was damp; the match went out just a second before; or the powder in the barrel was wet or defective in some way. The deer bounds away, and unless you are close to starving you go home, thinking that an Indian with a bow and arrow would have had a least two deer by this time.

Even in Europe the bow and arrow remained the principal hunting weapon until the invention of a better firing mechanism, the wheellock. This device eliminated the match, but it was intricate and expensive, so it never drove the matchlock from the scene. The wheellock, however, made possible the first genuine sporting guns, as opposed to weapons intended chiefly for war. It also provided a

firing mechanism for a mounted man, for whom the short harquebus was now fairly effective.

The wheellock introduced a new method of igniting powder in a gun—through sparks from iron pyrites, striking against rough steel. Some experts say it was invented by German gunmakers in Nuremberg, while others believe it was developed in Hungary or Italy. It never did reach many of the common people because it was too expensive. It became the essential lock on the sporting guns of Europe, but ·hunting in the main was confined to the upper classes, who owned the vast estates on which deer, wild boar, and other game roamed.

In the wheellock the bottom of the flashpan was cut out to admit the edge of a serrated steel wheel. The wheel was actuated by a

Many wheellocks were painstakingly fashioned and ornately decorated by the finest gunsmiths for the hunting aristocracy.

strong spring, with cogs that held it in place after it had been wound up. The flashpan was covered, but above it, in place of the old serpentine, was a small levered vise holding a piece of pyrites. In order to shoot the gun, one had to load and prime in the old manner, then wind up the wheel with a key or wrench. When the hunter pulled the trigger several things happened at once. The wheel began to whirl, the cover on the flashpan pulled to one side, the pyrites came down and touched the wheel. Sparks flew, igniting the priming powder which, through the touchhole, set off the main powder charge in the barrel. The trigger pull was hard because of the strength of the spring in the wheel.

The entire mechanism was built as a unit in what was called a lock, because of its resemblance to the common door locks of the time. It could be fitted to almost any gun with a touchhole in the side, and many matchlock harquebuses were converted to wheellocks for the hunting aristocracy. New guns were manufactured, beautifully fashioned and decorated by painstaking gunsmiths who had a fine sense of the artistic as well as a craftsmanship which was remarkable in view of the tools available to them. Some of the wheellock sporting guns made for kings and nobles

at that time are prized exhibits in many museums.

The wheellock, however, could not perform miracles. It actually did no more than eliminate the need for the match. The old methods of loading and priming remained, and the powder was as susceptible to dampness as ever. Indeed, the weapons of those days were still so unreliable that many were designed to serve a double purpose. Early pistols, for example, had butts topped with heavy balls of iron so the weapon could be used as a club when it failed to fire, or when an enemy came too close during the long period of reloading. There were harquebuses with sabers beneath the barrel; others with crossbows combined into the barrel and stock. Daggers were fitted into pistols, and even battle-axes on guns. Then came the bayonet, which really just made a firearm into a spear. The first of these plugged right into the end of the barrel, for the inventors calculated that once you reached the point of needing a spear the gun was useless. It was considerably later that the ring bayonet was worked out, making possible the use of a gun as a gun and also as a lance at close quarters.

In the middle of the sixteenth century the Spaniards developed the musket, a modification of the harquebus, to meet the need of

The elaborate wheellock mechanism (shown in cutaway view from left side) was operated by first winding the wheel lug on the opposite side with a "spanner," or wrench, three quarters of a turn (Fig. 1) which caused the chain links to raise the mainspring to a position of tension and cocked the trigger mechanism as the beveled head of the primary sear moved into the hole in the wheel under tension of the sear spring. When the trigger was pulled (Fig. 2), the primary sear was released from the notch in the secondary sear, and the force of the mainspring on the wheel pushed the beveled end of the primary sear out of the wheel hole, overpowering the sear spring. Simultaneously turned, the eccentric cam on the wheel moved the flashpan cover and the doghead moved down, throwing the pyrites against the serrated edges of the turning wheel, causing sparks in the flashpan.

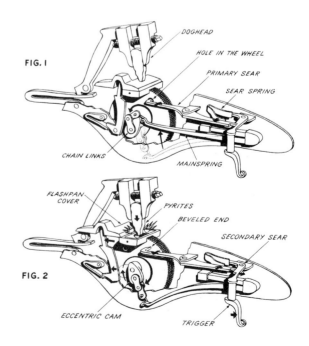

piercing the heaviest armor. Like some other cannons of its day, the musket took its name from European wildlife. "Musket" means a young male sparrow hawk, tiniest of the known hawks, and this gun was the smallest cannon. Since the Spanish wanted to equip large numbers of soldiers with this weapon, they used the inexpensive matchlock rather than the more costly and intricate wheellock. Originally, the musket was six to seven feet in length and weighed between forty and fifty pounds. The bullets it fired were heavy, weighing about an ounce and a half, and required a heavy charge of powder. Such a cumbersome weapon required a two-man crew to handle it, and it had to be fired from a rest. But the musket's range and accuracy were superior to the harquebus because of its longer barrel.

The musket was rapidly adopted by the other countries of Europe. Even England slowly began to replace the longbow with the musket as the gun was steadily changed and improved. Eventually the term "musket" came to be applied to guns quite different from the original small cannon of the Spaniards.

The sixteenth century was a period of great experimentation and improvement of firearms. Rifling, for example, was introduced in some gun barrels, probably first in Germany, well before 1550. The first rifling was straight, intended primarily to collect powder residue in the grooves and prevent fouling. But gunmakers had long believed that spiral rifling, which would give the bullet a spin as it left the barrel, could hold a ball to a truer course. The curving of feathers on arrows had proved the soundness of this principle. The first spiral rifling was done on wheellock harquebuses intended primarily for sport. But the difficulty of forcing a bullet down a rifled barrel so that it would fit tightly prevented the wide use of rifled guns for many years, although their power was often much greater than many of the smoothbores.

Gunmakers knew that rifling would be more practical if guns could be loaded from the breech (the rear end of the barrel), and many experiments were carried on in breech-loading mechanisms, which had already been used in heavy cannons. But it was impossible to prevent a strong leakage of gas at the breech until the expanding cartridge came along almost three hundred years later. Although museums contain numerous examples of early breechloaders, they were not widely used.

There were also efforts to make repeating firearms. One was a harquebus with a design which foreshadowed that of the modern revolver. It had a two-foot, nine-inch barrel, four rotating chambers, each seven and a half inches long, with a separate covered flashpan for each. Chambers and flashpans on this ingenious but unsightly weapon were arranged on a common cylinder rotated by hand. There was also a repeating matchlock which had six separate flashpans arranged one behind the other along the barrel, to fire six shots in succession. The mechanism had one serious flaw; touching off the first charge might explode all six—and the gun—at once.

One weapon developed in this period lasted considerably longer than many other experimental guns: the blunderbuss, which literally means "thunder gun," after the German "dunder buchse." Introduced by the Germans or the Dutch about 1510, this large-bore muzzle-loader had a flaring, funnel-shaped mouth and could fire either a handful of slugs or an assortment of nails, rocks, and similar odds and ends. Obviously precision aiming was not the goal, and a few specimens were fitted with wheellock firing mechanisms. But most were matchlock, and later flintlock, blunderbusses which were useful for frightening Indians or hunting flocks of sitting birds. English coachmen found the weapon handy to drive off highwaymen.

Then there was the German double horse pistol which, as its name indicates, could be carried by mounted men. It had over-and-under barrels, a significant new idea in gun-making which the Germans used again later in the century when they made a few double wheellock carbines.

Although there was much experimentation in Europe, the standard gun of the early American settler was the smoothbore matchlock musket, not the heavy, two-man Spanish musket requiring a rest but a descendant of that piece, light enough for one man to handle. It had a comparatively straight stock and simple lines, and its barrel—about four feet long—was bored to shoot balls weighing twelve to sixteen to the pound. There were also a few of the more expensive wheellocks, and some settlers brought along fowling pieces, which were the forerunners of the shotgun. As these developed, they were six and a half feet or more long, about 36 gauge, or a

Frenchmen exploring in Florida left a record of having killed "a crocodile" with "a gun," one of the first recorded kills with a firearm in the new world.

a half-inch in bore, and could fire small shot, two heavy slugs, or one large ball. It was probably with such a gun that the first recorded wing-shot was made by an unnamed Italian hunter in 1580. But it was many years before bagging a flying bird was anything but a rare and lucky event.

In view of the severe handicaps under which men hunted in those days, it is easy to see why the members of exploring parties in America were so enthusiastic whenever they scored a success with a firearm. The French under Captain Jean Ribault, an early navigator who investigated Florida, left a written record of killing "a crocodile" with "a gun." And an Englishman in Virginia about 1585 gave encouraging news to gunners back home when he wrote how the Indians hunted treed bears. "We too," he exclaimed, "have hunted them—and killed them with our muskets!"

CHAPTER 3

The Early Settlers and Their Weapons

The American colonists were eager for the guns that appeared as a result of the sixteenth century's great experimentation and progress in the development of firearms. The matchlock was cumbersome and undependable; the wheellock was intricate and expensive. A greatly improved mechanism was the snaphance (sometimes spelled snaphaunce), developed near the beginning of the sixteenth century, and the forerunner of the true flintlock, which was to become the universal means of ignition until the invention of the percussion cap in the early part of the nineteenth century.

Legend tells that the snaphance was first popularized by lawbreakers—Dutch chicken thieves, who were called *snap haans,* or hen snatchers. They could not afford wheellocks, and matchlocks betrayed their presence during nocturnal raids. So when the snaphance appeared—cheaper than the wheellock and without the matchlock's glowing rope—they welcomed it eagerly. While this is a pleasant tale, it is more likely, since *haan* means cock, that the term snaphance was suggested by the movement of the vise holding the flint, which resembles that of a pecking cock.

The snaphance used the familiar flint-against-steel method of striking sparks, without the expensive and delicate windup mechanism of the wheellock. The flint dropped sharply against a fixed "battery" of serrated steel, the sparks falling into the flashpan below to ignite the priming powder. At the same time, the trigger actuated a lever which moved the cover of the flashpan out of the way just before the flint fell. The gun's greatest asset, of course, was that it did away with the smoldering match, which so frequently went out at crucial moments and the acrid fumes of which warned game of the approach of the hunter.

Although the snaphance was rare in America, it was used successfully by some of the early settlers, one picturesque example being the bluff, rugged Myles Standish, military chieftain of the Plymouth Colony. He carried a snaphance when he led a party from the Mayflower on a hunting expedition on Cape Cod, even before the Pilgrims landed at Plymouth Rock. However, for several decades, before the snaphance developed into the true flintlock, the settlers were dependent almost entirely upon the matchlock.

During certain seasons of the year, at least, there was plenty of effective work for the weapon to do. As early as 1621 the settlers at

35

Plymouth enjoyed "great store of wild turkeys," ideal targets for the shot-scattering muzzle-loaders. Later, flocks of one hundred or more of the birds were reported; the gobblers ran big: there is mention of at least one sixty-pound giant. Flights of passenger pigeons—extinct today but so plentiful even in the late seventeenth century that they sold for a penny a dozen in Boston—darkened the sky; when a flock swooped down to land on a tree for a brief rest, it sometimes snapped off branches.

There were partridges, woodcock, quail, plover, snipe, and curlews. Captain John Smith of Jamestown Colony, with two companions, killed 148 ducks in one day, while others told of a sound of wings "like a great storm coming over the water." Wild swans and geese, which one waits for so impatiently today, were so numerous that no one tried to estimate their numbers.

And, of course, there were deer. From them the settlers obtained not only venison but, thanks to the teachings of friendly Indians, deerskins and bones from which to make tools. In the early days, many deer seemed unafraid of man—a fortunate thing in view of the short range of the settlers' muskets. In Virginia, herds of two hundred were sometimes sighted "close by the fort." Some pioneers hunted by setting fire to the woods and driving the deer toward an ambush—another technique learned from the Indians, who also showed them that

The snaphance mechanism used the flint-against-steel method of striking sparks. When the trigger was pulled, a lever was actuated to move the cover off the flashpan, then the flint dropped against a fixed battery of steel, causing sparks to fall into the flashpan and ignite the priming powder. Mechanism courtesy of Robert Abels, New York.

This Italian (Brescian) snaphance smoothbore with a folding butt was made in the seventeenth century. The snaphance was welcomed by the early Americans because it eliminated the need for the matchlock's glowing rope and cost much less than the wheellock. Gun courtesy of Metropolitan Museum of Art.

the bear could provide a warm skin, fat which the pioneers could use for soap and meat.

In some respects, no other animal could compare with the little beaver. His skin was the backbone of early trade and the center of many frontier squabbles. When the settlers discovered how highly beaver skins were valued back in Europe, they set out to collect all the flattails they could find, with no thought of conservation. It seemed impossible to think of wiping out the species or even diminishing the population seriously when a trapper could go out from Fort Orange (later Albany, New York) and gather four hundred beaver pelts in four or five weeks. The Dutch soon learned that they could gather more skins by buying them from the Indians who, lured by their desire for liquor and guns, forgot the sound teachings of their ancestors and went in for wholesale slaughter. Soon Dutch traders in New Amsterdam (later New York City) were handling fifteen thousand beaver skins a year, taken mostly by Indians of the Northeast. By 1633 the Iroquois alone carried thirty thousand beaver and otter skins to Fort Orange. Beaver skins became a common medium of exchange, the Dutch fixing the value of one skin at six guilders. (In Massachusetts, incidentally, musket balls were used instead of currency: one ball equaled a farthing.)

When supplies of skins began to decrease, trappers had to travel farther inland for the precious pelts. Many of them decided that it was easier to get the Indians to do the traveling, trapping, and hunting. But the Iroquois, for example, had cleaned out most of the beaver in their territory and had to poach on the hunting grounds of other tribes, who naturally resented the intrusion.

The Dutch, like other white settlers, tried to keep guns and powder out of the hands of the Indians. The redskins were no longer so friendly as they had been at first; when they learned that the white man wanted to take more and more of their land to clear and use for farms or towns, they often fought back. The settlers did not want them to have guns to help do that fighting, but the Indians were desperate for the protection these weapons would give. The Senecas, probably the toughest of all the Iroquois tribes, went directly to Governor Peter Stuyvesant of New Amsterdam. "We have a vast deal of trouble collecting beavers through the enemy country," they informed him. "We ask to be furnished with powder and ball. If our enemies conquer us, where then will ye obtain beaver?" The governor, knowing that the fur trade was of paramount importance to his superiors back in Holland, gave the Indians what they wanted, despite an earlier law of the colony prescribing the death penalty for anyone selling guns to the Indians. The law had never been enforceable, anway.

During the first year of the Jamestown settlement in Virginia, Captain John Smith threatened severe punishment to any Englishman found selling guns to the Indians. In Plymouth Colony, Governor William Bradford complained that one Thomas Morton— who had established a small colony at Merrymount, not far away—had shown the Indians how to use firearms and then hired them to hunt for him. In one way or another, Indians gradually obtained guns, and they paid high prices for them. The Mohawks, for example, paid "as many as twenty beaver" for any firearm the English would sell, and up to forty-five dollars a pound for powder, which often had been adulterated.

Because of the greed of many individuals and the rivalries of European nations about settlements in the New World, it was impossible to keep firearms out of the hands of the Indians. The Spanish, ruling Mexico with severity and strictness, forbade Indians to bear arms or ride horses; but when they tried to push northward into the Southwest and the Great Plains, they were resisted by Apache and Comanche Indians with guns. The guns had come from the English and the French, who did not want to see the Spaniards push their dominions too far into North America.

In the great struggle between the French and English, the French supplied guns to the Algonquin tribes, which were allied with them, while the English sold or—during actual wars—gave guns to their allies, the Iroquois.

Meanwhile, however, the white settlers had learned much from the Indians. They learned that the Indian method of fighting in the forest was better than methods they might have known in Europe—a knowledge that was to help them win a war later. The white man learned how to travel through the woods without heavy equipment, how to get the necessary food with his gun, how to sleep in the open, how to stalk and track. He learned from the Indian how to trap, fish, hunt, cook and enjoy the native foods such as maize and hominy. Most important, he learned how to make the birchbark canoe, which could carry him into the heart of the country.

Even after he had learned many of the ways of the Indian, the white settler starting off on a hunting or trapping expedition faced many trials and dangers. If he could come back to life today, he would be amazed at how easy hunting has become. True, he would also be astounded at how the swarms of wildlife he knew had dwindled. But compared with what

Wildfowlers braced guns against their thighs and shot all they could use of the plentiful supply of birds.

he went through to bag his game, today's hunting is simple.

The modern hunter sets out comfortably clad, while the early settler was not infrequently in rags. Today's hunter usually rides in comfort to the spot of his choice, while the pioneer hiked overland with a heavy load, hoping that he would not meet a band of hostile Indians. Once on the scene, the hunter of today has at his command a high-precision rifle or fast-shooting shotgun, both firing dependable ammunition. The settler struggled with his matchlock musket which gave him just one chance at his target. If he missed, he had to spend anywhere from three to ten minutes reloading, and by that time his quarry was usually far away. His weapon was pitifully inaccurate and limited in range. And in the early sixteen hundreds the stakes were high.

To provide meat for the table, teach Indians to stay off the warpath, and furnish a little incidental outdoor sport now and then, the settler had to rely on that crude gun of his. When it failed to fire, which was often enough to make even a mild-mannered Puritan angry, there was trouble. At best, that failure might mean an all-vegetable diet for a day or two. At worst, it might mean death by starvation or tomahawk. No matter how adept he became at handling his weapon, there were countless limitations that the colonist could not overcome.

It is not strange, therefore that the American settlers welcomed the flintlock so eagerly when it first became available. Here was a weapon that did away forever with the sometimes-glowing, sometimes-cold match, and replaced it with a mechanism that was simple, rugged, and fairly dependable.

The flintlock was a natural simplification of the snaphance and was developed in about 1610, in France, although it took somewhat longer for it to reach the New World. This lock functioned by forcing a piece of flint, set in viselike jaws, to strike against serrated steel and shower sparks into the flashpan to ignite the priming powder—which sounds just like the snaphance. But where the flashpan cover in the snaphance was a separate piece which was pushed out of the way by a lever connected to the trigger, the flashpan cover in the flintlock was an integral part of the steel "battery," which extended up from the cover. As the flint descended, it struck the rough steel and forced it back and away, exposing the open pan just in time for it to receive a shower of sparks.

The device was so rugged and trouble-free that flintlocks more than two hundred years old have been known to fire unerringly time after time. It is not surprising that the flintlock drove other firing mechanisms from the field within a few decades and that for a century and a half—until the introduction of percussion firing—it was the chief lock on firearms of all kinds: muskets, rifles, blunderbusses, fowling pieces, and pistols.

Only in some military circles was the flintlock looked upon with doubt. The British for a time made a combined match- and flintlock, and King Louis XIV of France forbade the use of the new weapon entirely. But as improvements were made in the lock's design, the armies of Europe joined sportsman and pioneer in adopting the new weapon. The American settlers found not only that the flintlock was more likely than other devices to fire in bad weather, but that it was also useful for striking fires in the wilderness.

Although the first flintlocks seen in this country varied widely, they averaged about five feet in length, with hammers close to three inches tall. One model, popular with many settlers and the Indians of New York, was about fifty inches long, of .50- to .60-caliber, with a full-length stock and brass sights. Such guns could be fired much more rapidly than earlier ones, so that the hunter had a better chance to get moving animals—or even make wing-shots, if he was an expert.

The American hunter of the middle of the seventeenth century considered himself lucky. He could "shoot the eye out of the wind" much better than his father, armed only with a matchlock musket during the early years in Jamestown or Plymouth. The flintlock secured the tenuous hold the early colonists had on the new land, and just as important, it led to the development of the first truly American firearm—the Kentucky rifle—which gave the frontier hunter new confidence to meet the challenge of the West.

A miss with a matchlock meant a minute or more to reload—while the deer bounded away.

CHAPTER 4

When New York City Was a Hunter's Paradise

New York City today is a huge area of hard pavements, towering skyscrapers, stone houses in unbroken rows—and a few parks in which the chief animal life consists of sparrows, pigeons, and squirrels. One does not expect to see a game bird or wild animal except in a zoo. Yet Manhattan Island, the heart of the city, was once a rich hunting ground.

Even the city seal offers evidence of the major role that wildlife once played in the life of the inhabitants. In the center, on a shield standing between an Indian and an early settler, are two beavers, the arms of a windmill, and two barrels. The windmill and the barrels represent New York's monopoly on packing and bolting flour for export, granted in 1678. But those beavers date back even further, to the fur trade which first led the Dutch to found New Amsterdam, which the English renamed New York when they took it over.

Before the coming of the white man, Algonquin Indians hunted and fished on the island. Although it was doubtless dotted with camps during the summer, the most secluded spot for winter rock shelters and bark lodges was at the northern tip of the island. It may be that the permanent headquarters of the Manhattan tribe were on the mainland. If so, these braves became, in effect, the first suburban commuters. Like other Indians of that period and general region, they dressed in deerskins and the leading belles decorated their arms with lynx skins. They led an easy life of fishing, hunting, and raising a few vegetables.

Their diet, the white men were shocked to learn, included eagles and such "similar trash" as bullfrogs, snakes, and tortoises. Worse yet, they rubbed fish oil, eagle fat, and coon grease on their skins. The concoction served to repel insects and as a kind of sun-tan lotion.

These were the natives first seen by Henry Hudson, English navigator and explorer then working for the Dutch, when he anchored in 1609 in what is now New York Harbor. But it was the wildlife that first attracted his attention. As his ship neared land, he sighted some herring gulls, red-breasted mergansers, and scoters, while close offshore were vast flocks of canvasbacks and redheads.

Exploring Manhattan Island, Hudson's men were delighted to see wood ducks, pintails, and mallards thronging the ponds. All around were belted kingfishers, great blue herons, American bitterns, loons, woodcock, Wilson's snipe, and songbirds of many kinds.

Across the wide river that now bears Hudson's name, hundreds of osprey bred in the cliffs of the Palisades. There were barred, screech, and great horned owls, countless ruffed grouse, bobwhites, geese, turkeys, pigeons, heath hens, nighthawks, and according to old accounts, pelicans and curlews. Underfoot were rattlers and other snakes.

The Indian chief who welcomed Hudson ordered two braves to shoot some birds for a feast. In what one chronicler reported as "the twinkle of an eye," the redskins were back with a staggering load of pigeons.

Animals were plentiful, too. Long after Hudson's time, it seldom took a man more than an hour to get his whitetail deer. Beavers, muskrats, minks, otters, martens, squirrels, red foxes, woodchucks, wolves, and rabbits abounded. The puma, Canada lynx, possum, and raccoon were not uncommon. Even ermine came near, and sometimes into, the area.

Hudson, quick to see the commercial possibilities of what he had found, reported to his Dutch employers that Manhattan Island would be an excellent place to start a fur-trading post. A year later a Dutch vessel laden with pelts left New Amsterdam, although it was several years before a tiny permanent post was established. By 1626 a typical ship's cargo included 7,250 beaver skins, 853 otters, 81 minks, 36 lynx, and 34 "small rats." In that same year Peter Minuit bought the whole island from the Indians for the now-famous trinkets valued at twenty-four dollars.

From the beginning, New Amsterdam was different from other white settlements in America. In the first place, it was founded by a commercial corporation—the Dutch West India Company—rather than the home govern-

Henry Hudson was welcomed by the Manhattan Indians when he landed in what is now New York harbor in 1609. For the occasion they prepared a grand feast using the island's plentiful supply of game and wildfowl.

ment. This company had been established frankly to prey on Spanish shipments of gold and silver, at which it was most successful; fur trading and colonization were mere offshoots of this primary activity. For many years the directors of the company vacillated between the idea of maintaining a trading post and that of putting down the firm roots of a lasting colony; for forty years fur trading was far more profitable and important than agriculture.

Since New Amsterdam was for so long primarily a trading center, it was a town in which one found a shifting population of trappers, traders, and sailors of many nationalities, by far the most cosmopolitan settlement in America. A Jesuit missionary reported in 1643 that he had heard eighteen different languages spoken on the streets of the little town. In time, of course, there were many good burghers from the old country who established themselves on Manhattan Island. They tried to build a small replica of the original Amsterdam, and they lived in reasonable comfort. They also had some leisure and the capacity to enjoy themselves, unlike early settlers in New England, who through rigorous necessity as well as their dispositions and beliefs, worked hard most of the time and frowned on frivolity.

The people of New Amsterdam had fun. They went sleighing, skating, and coasting in winter. They enjoyed hockey games, golf, bowling, and backgammon, among other amusements. Groups of friends went on picnics or hunting and fishing expeditions. Boys sharpened their eyes and skills with shooting contests, the most popular of which was shooting at the popinjay—a fowl hung by its feet from a tall pole.

The men naturally enjoyed hunting in this paradise of game, although they had their troubles. In 1626, the two hundred-odd mutton-loving settlers who lived near what is now the Battery at the lower tip of Manhattan, had trouble keeping wolves from devouring their small flocks of sheep. This problem solved itself; only a few years later, thanks to their

hunters, these same Dutchmen became so fond of venison that they no longer relished mutton.

By 1656, the population was only about one thousand, so there was still plenty of game close at hand. Some of them wrote glowing letters home about the sport they had with their crossbows, matchlock muskets, wheel-locks, and later their snaphances. One enthusiast, telling a friend about the game he had found, added, "If you will come hither with your family, you will not regret it." Another wrote that he had found a hunter's heaven, but that more men with firearms were needed to enjoy it properly. A third, after describing the waist-high grass that "serves to no other end except to maintain the deer, who can never devour a hundredth part of it," told his friends in the old country that anyone could get his fill of deer, turkey, goose, heath hen, crane, swan, duck, or pigeon in short order and could go fishing in either fresh or salt water.

Some early traders were harder to please. The shrilling birds made their heads ache, the racket of the wildfowl at night kept them awake, and the thousands of swans which made a thick "white napery" through which no one could see obscured their view of the Hudson River's western shore.

The Indians were helpful to the Dutch settlers. They gave them beans and corn, showed them how to fish and gather oysters, and initiated them into the lore of the wild. They taught them to burn the brush each spring and fall to eliminate crackling underfoot and make game easier to track. They demonstrated the art of driving deer to ambush, by setting fire to the woods and forcing the animals to a narrow ambush where they were easily killed.

Another Indian deer-driving technique, which the Dutch were reluctant to use, involved a chain of braves, each a hundred paces from his neighbor and armed with a deer's thigh bone and a stick. At a signal from the leader, the chain advanced, beating bones and sticks together and driving the frightened deer toward the water surrounding the island. Hunters concealed on the shore killed most of the creatures with bows and arrows, and those that jumped into the water were either roped and drowned or overtaken by hunters who jumped in after them, grabbed them by the ears, and steered them back to be killed.

The Dutch also learned from the Indians how easily passenger pigeons could be killed, with the result that some years later these fine game birds became extinct. Flying north, they reached the present New York area each April. Like the partridges, they actually darkened the sky, and flew so low that the Indians killed thousands merely by throwing stones and clubs into the air. The Dutch, with their cross-bows and firearms, did much to speed this wholesale slaughter.

Soon after the great pigeon flight—a holiday event in nearly every settlement along the flyway—the northbound geese and ducks started to arrive, seeking shelter in the Hudson River-Newark Bay region off the west shore of Manhattan. When the thousands of birds settled on the water, they were so closely packed and so unafraid of man that they offered easy targets even for the crude muzzle-loaders of those early days. One old account tells of eleven gray geese taken with one shot, and it was reported that the average gray goose weighed sixteen pounds.

Fish swarmed in the salt waters surrounding the island and in the fresh-water streams and ponds which dotted it from shore to shore. Before the white man came to Manhattan, the local Indians bartered tons of fish with inland tribes. Their fishing gear included barbless hooks of bone; gill nets of woven bark-fiber cord held upright by small sticks and weighted by notched pebbles; bows and arrows, and cedar-pronged spears about twelve feet long. Sometimes two braves worked together at night in a canoe, one tending a small fire built

on a hearth at the middle of the canoe and the other at the bow or stern, propelling the craft with the butt of his spear. The navigator could then use the sharp end of the spear on any fish he spied motionless in the water, spellbound by the blaze. Other Indians used a torch or firebrand fastened to the bow as the jacklight.

Shad, cod, herring, striped bass, salmon, perch, and pike were common. So was the sturgeon, a staple food which came to be called "Albany beef" because its spawning grounds were near that town on the upper Hudson. The Dutch used numbers instead of names for some fish. They called the shad "eleven," because they claimed that it appeared without fail each year off Sandy Hook on March 11. The striped bass was "twelve," because it had six stripes on each side. Smelt were "breakfast fish," because the Dutch ate so many of them morning after morning, with patties of venison and other game.

A major landmark in old New York, bordering on a downtown stretch of what is now Broadway, was spring-fed Fresh Water Pond. It was the home of several species of fish, and game birds—especially snipe and woodcock—frequented its shores. The Indians dried fish on an island in its center, away from prowling animals and possibly hostile groups. Their children, often accompanied by Dutch boys playing hooky from school, had their best sport fishing in the millrace far downtown, using homemade hooks of birds' claws, chicken bones, and locust thorns.

The Dutch settlers enjoyed their hunting and fishing and from the first insisted on their right to make use of the natural resources they found around them. Since New Amsterdam was more or less a "company town," they insisted that in the original draft of the "freedoms and exemptions for New Netherland" specific permission be granted for "fishing and hunting in public woods and streams." The

Predators abounded on Manhattan Island and found farmers' flocks easy prey, since the best firearm was the single-shot, muzzle-loading flintlock.

aristocratic patroons were guaranteed "fishing, hunting, and fowling rights" on their large estates.

The law required every householder to have powder, lead, and a firearm that had been inspected and approved. The Dutch bought their shot at a small general store which sold everything from linen and hooks and eyes to "suggar candy." And at least once the authorities in Holland, receiving a requisition for sixty muzzle-loaders, a package of flints, a parcel of "match," twelve hundred pounds of powder, and two thousand pounds of lead, were bluntly given to understand that this was not only for defense but for "hunting and fowling" as well.

For their sport, many of the Dutch at first favored the crossbow rather than the matchlock or wheellock. Their most popular hunting arm, the snaphance, came later, and by the time the English took over Manhattan in 1664, the flintlock was in general use.

At first there was rarely any need to go beyond what is now the Wall Street area on lower Manhattan for good hunting. But in time the hunters pushed north, beyond the deep pits dug to trap marauding wolves (for whose hides there was a bounty) and on to the region just below Fourteenth Street which has come to be known as Greenwich Village. Since hunting played a major role in the life of the community, many landlords recognized the fact in their business dealings. In 1639, for example, a Dutch preacher signed a lease for a Manhattan "plantation" along with "a water dog, gun, and powder at a certain rent payable in tobacco, and one third of all the game [the lessee] shall kill, as long as the powder and ball last."

Not all hunters hiked north for their hunting. There was still shooting in the little town itself. In 1652, officials complained that "many guns" were fired daily within the town at partridges and other game, and warned that this practice must stop. Anyone violating the regulation would lose his gun and pay a heavy fine, one third of which would go to the poor, another to the church, and the balance to the arresting officer. A few years later "several persons, both white and coloured," were fined for "shooting pigeons in the woods on Sunday, contrary to ordinance." Also, hog hunting in the public woods of Manhattan without a permit was forbidden. Even so, still more teeth were needed in the laws, for overeager game-bird hunters persisted in ruining gardens and fences, according to protests which have a familiar ring today.

For years the game was so plentiful that it was tempting for hunters to ignore regulations and personal property. One diarist reported seeing a Dutchman bring down thirty-four pigeons with a single blast, and eighty-four starlings (called maize thiefs because they stole the ripe corn around Nassau Street) killed with one shot "in the commander's orchard." "They taste good," he added. Other accounts tell of a one-shot artist bagging eleven prairie hens, and of an Englishman shooting in a few hours more than a hundred of these birds in the area south of the present Times Square.

A gala annual event, usually held near Christmas, was the turkey shoot. The wild birds, frequently traveling in flocks of five hundred, weighed from thirty to forty pounds each. Sometimes, as they landed from one of their short flights, the Indians would grab turkeys with their bare hands. The Dutch shot the birds from trees at dusk, hunted them with dogs, and even captured them by "angling" with baited hooks.

The turkey shoots of later days were generally held on an ice-covered swamp near what is now Park Row and the end of the Brooklyn Bridge. Each contestant paid six to ten cents in advance for his shot at a bird, and the man who scored a direct hit got his bird for very little. In the words of one early account, "If he hit it so as to draw blood, it was his for a Christmas or New Year dinner."

Hunting within the present New York City

limits was not confined to Manhattan. Across the Harlem River was the game-filled Bronx, much of which was originally included in Jonas Bronck's farm, from which the borough took its name. On Long Island were two more areas destined to form a part of the metropolis: Brooklyn, where deer were scarce because of wolves and wildcats; and Queens, where in 1726 the foxes and wildcats became so numerous and bothersome that measures were taken to destroy them. To the southwest, nowadays half an hour's ferry ride from Manhattan, was

Staten Island, where an English governor once went bear hunting when he should have been presiding at a council meeting in the city.

On Manhattan itself, in 1755, an Englishman asleep in a thicket was shot by mistake. The hunter thought he had spotted a bear. A large black bear was killed in the waterfront region four years later, and the "bear market," opened in 1771 inside the city limits, got its name because someone shot a bear near by. Soon the butcher who ran the store was selling bear meat in quantity and had no trouble finding market hunters to maintain his supply.

Wildcats were the first predators to be eliminated from the New York area. They were so commonly encountered that harassed settlers organized hunts to exterminate the beasts. By 1780, when a flintlock marksman shot a wildcat robbing hen roosts only a mile from the center of town, that rare event was news.

Where Dutch boys once went fishing with their Indian friends, towering skyscrapers now overlook the bustling, hurrying crowds of New York City.

In 1822, sportsmen were hunting marshland snipe where Twenty-third Street and Seventh Avenue now intersect, and even in 1830 the city north of Fourteenth Street was described as a "partial wilderness," with only a few country mansions and a few rough roads. Fresh Water Pond had been filled in, but there were still fish and beaver in the clear-running streams that trickled east or west from the long north-south ridge which became Broadway. To get a bear, wolf, deer, beaver, fox, or raccoon, the hunter had only to hike up beyond what later became 125th Street.

Although the city kept growing, wildlife contested every foot of the white man's advance. The inhabitants could not believe that so much game could ever disappear, but their unrestrained hunting and the efficient work of market hunters hastened the inevitable end of New York as a game area. Wild turkeys disappeared, as did another fine and once-common bird, the heath hen. Its numbers had dwindled alarmingly by 1708, so New York adopted a closed season to protect it. But closed seasons were hard to enforce in those days, and by 1840 the heath hen was listed as extinct on Long Island, once its chief home.

The problem of how to punish careless hunters was to plague the City Council as late as 1829. Shortly after the turn of the century, in prohibiting "the practice of fowling in the public streets," the Council gave the mayor power to hire marshals to enforce the law. In 1813, a youth caught shooting a gun in Greenwich Village was jailed when he refused to pay his fine. The following year, when gunsmith Jeremiah Yooman asked to be assigned a place within the city limits where he might prove his rifles, the Council's action was coldly noted in the records, "Resolved: That the petitioner have leave to withdraw his petition."

In the second half of the nineteenth century, sportsmen ceased to be a problem, for though much of the far-uptown section remained rural, hunting on Manhattan had come to an end. The easy days when Indians sold "stores" of venison at the door for ninepence was just a memory, and the wildlife in the New York area was disappearing forever.

In its place today are millions of birds, the descendants of fourteen "European sparrows" liberated in Central Park in 1863. Beaver Street, once the site of a beaver dam and later a busy fur-trading center, is now merely one of a network of paved thoroughfares. Springs no longer bubble along Spring Street. Water Street has lived down its reputation of being frequently submerged. Greenwich Village, long a favorite gunning spot, has become an area of night clubs and apartments. Sections where the partridges once thundered as they took off are jammed with tenements and taxis, overlooked by skyscrapers, and packed with city dwellers.

That is New York, once a wilderness hunting ground, now the nation's largest city.

CHAPTER 5

The Battle with the Wolves

Confined to the protection of America's national forests, the wolves of the continental United States numbered fewer than three thousand in the middle of the twentieth century. This is a mere handful compared to the two million or more wolves that once ranged over almost every region in the early days of the country's development. The wolf is no longer a national problem, but in the seventeen hundreds, when the colonists were struggling to establish their homes and farms and push back the wilderness, he was a major threat.

Described as "unscrupulous," "despicable," and "bloodsucking," the wolf was hated in every settlement along the Eastern seaboard. He slaughtered sheep and cattle, killed valuable dogs, and it has been said that he even attacked humans. The war the colonists waged against him was a showdown battle with no rules. And when the smoke had cleared, the wolf, still snarling defiance and more cunning than ever, had been pushed back from the settlements. But the toll he had taken was a heavy one.

The wolf started his depredations long before the white man even dreamed that North America existed. Some Indians ate wolf meat.

A few succeeded in taming wolf puppies and using them as dogs, but most Indians looked upon the wolf as a crafty, intelligent, and ruthless foe. Indian folklore is filled with tales of ferocious wolves. When the wolf came into contact with the colonists, however, he found the scales tipped against him for one big reason: these men had firearms.

At first, because most of the settlers had not used arms in Europe and because the weapons they brought with them were slow and undependable, the wolf came dangerously close to annihilating the colonies' sheep and cattle. As time went on, however, the descendants of the first colonists became American sharpshooters, thoroughly skilled with rifle, smoothbore musket, or fowling pieces.

The introduction and steady improvement of the flintlock, which, in one fast motion of the hammer, knocked the cover from the flashpan and sent a shower of sparks flying into its powder, helped give the colonists the edge they needed over the wolf. One gun of that period, described as an "elegant combination military and sporting piece," was five feet, nine inches long with a barrel four feet, five and a half inches long, a caliber of thirteen-sixteenths of an inch, and weight of fifteen

Wolf scalps, with bounty due on them, circulated freely as currency in almost every colony.

pounds. These are no more than examples, for all firearms varied considerably and many were made to the specifications of the purchaser.

A few flintlock rifles were imported from England in the seventeen hundreds, but they were not widely used until German and Swiss immigrants, around Lancaster, Pennsylvania, began to make rifles to fit the needs of the frontier. Their weapons evolved in time into the famous Kentucky rifle, discussed in Chapter Six.

Before the wolf retreated westward, he played a crucial part in early American history. To the colonists he was a pest, a menace, and an enemy. But they met him head-on. The struggle between them was one of the most decisive that Americans have won. Cunning and clever, the wolf pounced on the livestock of Jamestown, Virginia, as soon as it was introduced in 1609. In the years that followed he struck at almost every settlement along the Atlantic Coast.

Sheep were his specialty. The first settlers found these animals so hard to defend with their slow-firing, short-range muskets that within a few decades English travelers reported that they rarely observed flocks of more than twenty sheep. In Vermont, roaming packs of predators often killed whole flocks. Female wolves even stole the pups of farm dogs to feed to their young. And in Virginia, where farmers often kept several dogs to guard their sheep, mutton soon became more of a treat than any wild game.

Within a few years bounty laws were passed in almost every colony. In some places, payments equaled the budget for all other purposes. Some settlements paid off in wine, others in tobacco, and still others in grain, sheep, rum, hogs, powder, and lead. Virginia, whose laws forbade the shooting of wild hogs in the forests, promised in 1632 that anyone bringing in a wolf's head would have the privilege of killing one pig. Marylanders used wolf scalps, on which bounty payments were due, as currency. Wolf skins had considerable value, too. In some places they were used as blankets, while in others Indians would pay up to forty beaver skins for the pelt of a black wolf. The natives believed that such a skin, worn as a coat, could cure the aches and pains of old age. Sometimes a chief would present a black-wolf pelt to the leader of a neighboring tribe in an effort to patch up a misunderstanding.

Bounty payments varied from year to year and from one colony to another. In 1642 the wolves became so bad in Rhode Island that hunters were hired by the day to kill them off. Massachusetts paid bounties according to the method used by the hunter—forty shillings to anyone employing hounds, ten shillings for bagging a wolf any other way. The officials wanted to encourage the keeping of hounds capable of killing wolves. They went even further later by decreeing that any man owning suitable dogs would not be subject to the tax levied on domestic animals. Eight years later the General Assembly gave to the selectmen of each town the authority to requisition and board such dogs, and to exclude from the town any dog that did not meet their approval. Massachusetts also offered successful wolf-hunting Indians a choice of rewards for each wolf killed: two pounds of powder and eight pounds of shot; or one pound of powder, four pounds of shot, and five shillings in corn "or other pay"; or a straight ten shillings.

Despite the bounties, the wolf still deterred livestock farming. As late as 1717, the Cape Cod area of Massachusetts seriously considered building wooden fences more than six feet high around the settlements just to keep out wolves. This proposal was defeated because towns outside of the projected barriers complained that the wolves would be directed to concentrate on them.

The colonists knew that they could never farm in peace so long as wolves were near. Typical of the plaintive notes left in the diaries, letters, and reports of those times are some records from North Carolina in the mid-eighteenth century. One settler wrote in 1752 that it was useless to try to raise cattle until the wolves and bears were wiped out. The settlement, this chronicler noted, had an abundance of local game but was sadly in need of hunters to bring in the meat. A short time later he wrote that the settlers had killed ten pigs because it cost too much to feed them while they were kept in pens, and they could not be allowed to forage because of the wolves. He added dolefully, "The wolves have killed many of our calves this spring."

Like most settlements, this one soon acted to meet the problem by building wolf pits. These were large holes, varying in size, placed in strategic locations. They averaged perhaps ten feet in depth, with sides overhanging so sharply that in some cases the top was five feet wide and the bottom thirty feet wide. Sharp stakes were driven into the ground at the bottom to impale the wolf as he fell. Some pits had tipping platforms of small branches, fastened to axles of heavy timber and baited with venison. Others used sheep as bait, tying the animal to a tall pole or placing him on a mound of earth in the center of the pit.

Perhaps the best instructions for digging such a pit came from an early settler who said that it should be so deep and steep that the wolf "can no more scramble out again than a husband who has taken the leap can scramble out of matrimony."

The Puritans' strict ideas of morality did not prevent them from torturing wolves. Predators caught in pits were often tied to nearby posts and baited by fierce dogs or, while still alive, were dragged for miles behind a horse. Others were driven into holes or stockades and shot by gunners posted along the top. Still other were caught on mackerel hooks tied together in a bunch and dipped in tallow. A dead carcass was used to lure the wolf to the hooks.

The early settlers also used snares, traps, and deadfalls—most of them borrowed from the Indians. The deadfalls usually consisted of three notched sticks, arranged in a figure 4,

with a heavy weight so suspended that when a wolf pulled at the bait of the horizontal strip he caused the weight to fall on him. Other pioneers, pushing on into the forests, tried to destroy the wolves by poisoning them with strychnine placed in dead sheep or other bait.

Some settlers used their firearms in wolf traps. Set guns, so arranged that a tug at the bait pulled the trigger, were in use as early as 1650. Since such devices could be dangerous traps for human beings, the General Court at Easthampton, Long Island, ruled that they were illegal within a half mile of town and

The deadfall trap consisted of three notched sticks arranged in a figure 4 so that when a wolf touched the bait, a heavy log fell on him.

could not be left out after sunrise.

Individual hunters, barefoot and lightly garbed in summer but warmly wrapped in homemade fabrics in winter, fought the wolf without respite. Communities organized drives. Ring hunts, which set a pattern followed today in some Western areas for jack rabbits and coyotes, consisted usually of a circle of hunters who converged on a central point, driving all game and predators before them. Sometimes the woods or brush were fired to help drive the animals as the hunters closed in. The main trouble with such methods, according to one participant, was that too many trigger-happy pioneers shot each other instead of the wolves.

As weapons improved, however, more settlers found that they could abandon such mass techniques and go after the wolf with their more accurate flintlocks, which could, in the hands of a good marksman, hit a moving target—even the fleet wolf. This kind of shooting gave invaluable training to the American farmers and frontiersmen who first saved many British regulars in the French and Indian Wars and then outshot and outfought them in the Revolution. When British General Braddock marched thirteen hundred redcoats into an Indian trap in Pennsylvania while fighting the French, George Washington's farmer-riflemen, firing Indian style from behind rocks and trees, managed to save some four hundred of the frantic regulars. The same tactics were turned against the British in 1776, although only a handful of the Continental troops carried rifles. Thus the wolf, against whom the settlers fought so grimly, helped train the marksmen who were to win America's freedom.

The gray raider also helped establish the reputation of Israel Putnam, "Old Put," who was later to become a major general in the Continental Army. In the area of Pomfret, Connecticut, where Putnam had his farm, there was a particularly troublesome female wolf whose livestock raids had cost the residents dearly. Putnam was one of six farmers who agreed to take turns hunting her until she was destroyed.

One night the wolf struck at Putnam's farm, killing seventy-five sheep and goats, and injuring several lambs and kids. After a long, twisting chase a pack of hounds drove the wolf into her den a few miles from Putnam's place. For twelve hours the farmers and townspeople, armed with rifles and smoothbore muskets, tried to drive the beast out by setting fires around the den and forcing smoke and sulphur fumes into it. An hour or two before midnight, when all efforts had failed, Putnam volunteered to go in alone and kill the animal.

Fastening a long rope around his legs so that he could signal when he wanted to be pulled out, he seized a birchbark torch and entered the den, a long rock cave about three feet wide and not much higher. Crawling slowly on hands and knees, he finally sighted the wolf at the far end of the cave, gnashing its teeth and growling. The crowd outside, alarmed at the growls, yanked swiftly on the rope, and Putnam came sliding out, his shirt pulled over his head and his flesh cut and bruised.

Catching his breath, he loaded his weapon with nine buckshot, took the torch in his other hand, and again crawled the forty-foot length of the sloping cave. This time the wolf was crouching, ready to spring. Putnam took aim at her head and fired. The roar and smoke of the gun stunned him, and before he could get his bearings he was again yanked out of the cave. He waited until the smoke had cleared away and then went inside to claim his victim.

Although the wolf helped give Putnam his reputation and sharpened the shooting eyes of the men who were to become his soldiers, it also helped to undermine morale in the Revolutionary Army. Farmers' wives, forced to defend even the pigpens against middle-of-the-night raids by wolf packs, complained that their livestock was being wiped out. They wrote to their husbands, off fighting the war,

Farm wives sometimes had to protect livestock from wolves with pitchforks while their husbands were away at war.

begging them to come home before all the cattle, sheep, and pigs were destroyed. Some women even wielded pitchforks in their close-quarters battles with wolves. One shot three that were attacking her watchdog. Another woman, according to legend that may have been exaggerated with the passing of years, killed a particularly nasty specimen by hitting him over the head with a Dutch oven!

Immediately after the Revolution the cries of wolf packs near some stables along the frontier frightened horses so badly that they were useless the next day. In some places, farmers or their wives who went to the barns to tend the animals in the evening might be cut off from their houses by a pack of wolves and able to return only after daybreak.

In the early days of Pennsylvania, packs of five hundred wolves were sighted. In 1812, a man reported having been followed by two hundred of them. As late as 1820 a business-man failed in his woolen-goods mill at Dingmans Ferry, Pennsylvania, because his sheep were killed off by wolves. George Washington and Thomas Jefferson spoke and wrote with feeling of the wolf problem in Virginia in the closing years of the eighteenth century.

It is therefore not surprising that professional wolf hunters flourished in America. Bill Long, born near Reading, Pennsylvania, in 1790, was credited with killing two thousand wolves, many of which he lured from the forest by calling to them—a trick he learned from the Indians. A little later, ten-year-old Jim Jacobson, who grew up to be a famous hunter, killed one of the biggest wolves known in Pennsylvania. Alone in a cabin for the day, the boy went out in the snow to look at a "calf" he had sighted near a brook. Closer inspection showed the calf to be a wolf, which chased him back to the cabin. Jacobson got his father's gun, quietly opened the window, and fired at the wolf, which was still sniffing at the doorstep.

The bullet hit the animal's jugular vein, killing it almost instantly. Subsequent examination revealed that the hundred-pound wolf measured six feet, one inch, from "tip to tip," and had a tail two feet long.

Not many wolves were killed so easily, however. They learned the ways of man and how to meet his tricks so successfully that many hunters came to temper their dislike of the creatures with admiration for their craftiness. One trapper, trying to outwit a wily wolf, arranged a live trap six feet long, with the front raised three feet above the ground. Then

he baited it. The wolf burrowed under the floor and pulled the bait safely through the cracks.

Next, the man tried a trap shaped like a funnel, but the wolf refused to enter it. The next device was a double-spring trap, with only the bait uncovered. The wolf left tracks all around but again spurned the trap. Finally, the hunter hung pieces of meat, on separate strings, along a tree limb, with one tempting morsel suspended directly over a trap. When he returned, he found every piece of meat gone except the one that would have caught the

Israel Putnam, later a Revolutionary general, won early renown when he entered a dark, narrow cave and killed a Western timber wolf in a close-quarter battle.

wolf. The trapper gave up that particular struggle.

Other men combined the old fishhook idea with that of the hanging meat. They concealed three cod hooks, tied back to back, in each piece of meat, which was suspended several feet above the ground from a strong limb. When the wolf jumped to get the bait, he was hooked.

Because the battle against the wolf was so intense, it is now difficult to decide where facts end and folklore begins. There is, for example, the story of a hunter who reported in 1788 that he had killed four wolves with one shot—a "heavy bullet" from a muzzle-loader allegedly passing through the throats of four lined-up animals. Later, there was mention of a hunter who was out to get a wolf that had been raiding his stock. Carefully he followed the animal's tracks into a ravine, where six wolves suddenly attacked him. The theory advanced was that these wolves had purposely been marching single file, stepping in each other's tracks as they went along, to deceive anyone following them.

In the early eighteen hundreds, the wolf was hunted for sport in a few localities, notably on the upper Mississippi River and around Chicago, much as the beast had once been hunted by the horseback-riding young blades of pre-Revolutionary Virginia. Specially shod horses raced over the ice of the northern Mississippi, chasing wolves, which usually could be overtaken and killed at the end of about four miles. Dogs, however, were often outwitted in such chases by smart wolves who would run straight to an air hole, carefully trot along the edge to the opposite side, and then resume their course. The dogs, intent on the fleeing wolf, would plunge into the hole, ending the chase with an unexpected swim. Some enthusiasts kept packs of staghounds and greyhounds to chase wolves at night over dry land and kill the predators when they finally caught them.

But most wolf-hunting was a matter of grim necessity. The predators were a serious threat to the early settlers, who used every resource to get rid of them. The early Americans cleared the Eastern seaboard, pushing the wolf before them. Years later, when the flintlock had given way to powerful rifles, the wolf made another stand in the West. But again, all his wiles and his knowledge of man's tricks failed to save him.

CHAPTER 6

The Kentucky Rifle

The first truly American firearm was the Kentucky rifle. For more than a century it was universally conceded to be the world's best, and it established records that still command respect. The Kentucky rifle was a picturesque arm—long, graceful, and accurate in both hunting and warfare. Its importance in opening up large areas of the United States cannot be overestimated. It played a decisive role in many battles of the Revolutionary War; it may even be true that one long-range hit by a Kentucky rifle turned the tide in that war and led to the nation's independence.

Let us take a close look at this fabulous weapon. For one thing, its name is not accurate. The earliest models were made in Pennsylvania for pioneers, many of whom then pushed on into Kentucky, the name then given to the wilderness beyond the Cumberland Mountains. Thus the rifle was named for the region in which it was first used, not where it was first made. Later, these weapons were fabricated in small shops as far west as St.

Louis, along the Ohio River, and in Tennessee, Virginia, the Carolinas—and Kentucky. But many men spoke of their Pennsylvania, not Kentucky, rifles, and some European firearms authorities still prefer to call them "American rifles."

Another misleading point should be cleared up. Not all so-called Kentucky rifles were true rifles. Many of them were made with smooth bores, and some had straight rather than spiral rifling. The majority, however, were rifled to give about one complete turn to the bullet as it moved down the length of the barrel.

The most important point about the Kentucky rifle, and the reason for its great success, was that it was developed in direct response to America's needs, especially the needs of men living on the frontier. Muskets had been improved, of course, and the flintlock had made them far more reliable than the old matchlocks, but they were heavy and their range was short. The rifles that had been imported from Europe were of little more value in the American wilderness. An example is the German Jaeger, some of which were brought to the colonies by the very German and Swiss immigrants who later developed the earliest Kentuckys.

The Jaeger was a highly respected weapon on the European continent, having been used widely in both German and Austrian armies. It was considerably shorter than the average flintlock musket, with a heavy barrel that shot .75-caliber balls. Such bullets needed heavy powder charges to propel them. But the worst feature of the Jaeger was the difficult loading. In a rifled barrel, any ball that would fit easily allowed "windage," or escape of the propelling gases, through the grooves. In order to seal the bullet tightly in the barrel, it had to be as large as the bore of the grooves. Pounding such a ball home required a metal rod and a mallet. Moreover, as the lands (the ridges between the rifling grooves) cut into the lead of the bullet they distorted it so that its flight was often erratic. Loading Jaegers was lengthy and noisy—two great disadvantages in the woods, whether one expected game or Indians. The design of the Jaeger was ugly and ungainly; trigger guards were bulky yet easily broken; sights were useless in dark forests or in any spot where accuracy was vital. Such guns could never offer serious competition to the smoothbores.

That was the state of affairs in the seventeen twenties when frontiersmen in the vicinity of Lancaster, Pennsylvania, began complaining to the newly arrived German and Swiss gunsmiths there. These immigrants were steeped in the traditions of their homelands, where they had heard even the simple flintlock opposed because the smiths wanted to retain the more expensive wheellock firing mechanism. But in response to the demands of obstinate frontiersmen who knew exactly what they wanted, the famous Kentucky model evolved. It hit its stride about 1730, but underwent steady changes for many years. Most rifles were built to the individual buyer's specifications or according to the maker's latest experiments, and the resulting new ideas were eagerly seized upon by competing smiths. For this reason, surviving examples show wide variations in detail.

No frontiersman wanted to carry a heavy weapon on his long treks in the wilderness. The weight of the Kentucky was steadily reduced until the average hunting rifle weighed between nine and ten pounds. Those made for match shooting averaged about nineteen pounds. The caliber was reduced from the .65 to .75 common in Europe to about .45, so the pound of lead that once yielded sixteen bullets now gave forty-eight .45-caliber balls—three times as many chances for fresh meat or shots at hostile Indians. The man on the frontier did not need bullets larger than .45, for he had no armor to pierce. With smaller bore and bullets, he needed much less powder for the same number of shots. The front sight of the Kentucky was enlarged and the trigger guard strengthened while it was stripped of its bulk.

Probably the most distinctive change came in the barrel, which on earlier rifles had been generally short and heavy. Now it was lengthened, so the gun measured in early

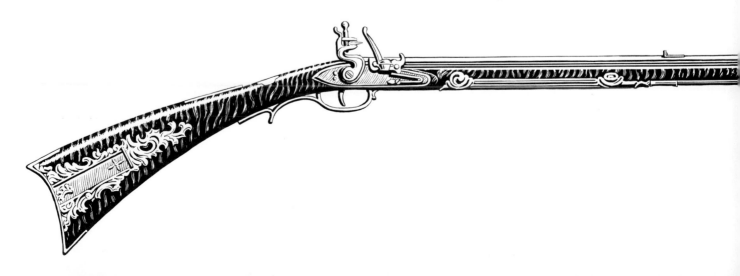

models from fifty-one to seventy-seven inches, or sometimes almost triple the length of the average big-game rifle of today. This meant that less powder was needed than before, for it burned cleaner. In the opinion of many authorities, the Kentucky's long barrel, which gave greater accuracy at the same time that it deadened the noise of firing, was the main factor in the success of this weapon.

But perhaps another factor was just as important—the patch method of loading, invented by some unknown genius but first used widely with the Kentucky rifle. Thanks largely to this discovery, rifles could be reloaded in one-fourth the time it took before, and eventually backwoodsmen were getting off their second shots in less than half a minute after the first.

To patch-load a rifle, you cast the lead-ball bullet in a mold three-hundredths of an inch smaller than the actual caliber demanded. In loading, you slipped a piece of dressed buckskin or a bit of old felt, about the size of a fifty-cent piece and well greased with tallow, under the ball as you held it over the muzzle. Then, when you rammed the ball down the barrel, the greased patch helped it slide along easily, doing away with the noisy hammering. Moreover, the grooves of the rifling cut into the patch, which made a tight seal, and not into the bullet, which remained undistorted.

These developments did not come at once. They were spread over many years, but if it were possible to describe a "typical" or composite Kentucky rifle, it might be approximately like this:

Its forty-two-inch barrel, usually a full octagon, gave the .45-caliber rifle an over-all length of about fifty-five inches. The stock, which extended to the muzzle, was of curly maple, occasionally cherry or, in the South, apple wood. The buttplate was crescent-shaped rather than straight. In the right side of the stock a long, narrow box was cut into the wood for carrying the greased patches. The box cover was made of brass, and was often elaborately decorated. The left side of the stock was often carved to make a comfortable cheekpiece and contained a metal ornament, usually of simple design. The rifle's forty-four to fifty parts were handmade and not interchangeable. Many Kentuckys made liberal use of brass on the side plates, buttplate, front sight, rod pipes or thimbles, and trigger guard, as well as on the patch box. But most hunting models lacked decorations, because these might reflect the sun and frighten game, or often the fancy touches were too costly for the frontiersman.

Although the early locks, or firing mechanisms, were homemade, those for many of the later models were imported from Germany or England. The British usually supplied the flints, which sold for two cents each and were good for fifty shots.

To give a stock an artificial "curly" or "fiddleback" grain, the maker wound tarred string around the wood and then burned it off. Soot and oil were rubbed in to stain the wood, and some stocks were treated with a special oil varnish. All in all, the Kentucky was made well, even though some models sold for only twelve to fourteen dollars in contrast to a hundred and twenty-five dollars for a fancy European sporting smoothbore. The Kentucky

The Kentucky rifle was developed in response to the needs of the American frontiersman. Its longer, lighter barrel made it more accurate and easier to handle than previous guns.

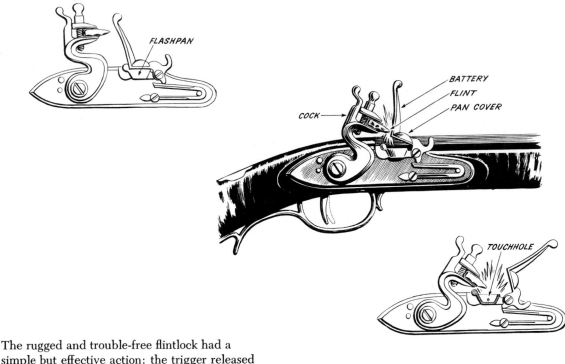

FLASHPAN

BATTERY
FLINT
PAN COVER

COCK

TOUCHHOLE

The rugged and trouble-free flintlock had a
simple but effective action: the trigger released
the cock holding the flint, allowing it to pivot
forward. As the flint descended, it struck the
rough steel of the battery and forced it
back, exposing the open pan just in time
to receive a shower of sparks.

was a gun for the common man, the independent and self-reliant man.

Exposure, rust, and the constant wear on the barrel from use of the split-hickory ramrod eventually forced many owners to return their rifles to the smith for "freshing" or enlarging of the caliber. This meant the hunter had to use larger patches or ream out his old mold to cast bigger bullets. Some worn rifles were refinished as smoothbores.

Although legend would have us believe that every frontiersman was a crack shot—and a great many were indeed expert marksmen—some users of the Kentucky rifle were not so skillful. With such men, the Kentuckys with straight-cut rifling were popular, for they

made good combination arms. These guns could fire two lead balls at once, as the smoothbore could, or even handle loads of BB to No. 4 shot. Yet they would fire a single patch and ball accurately enough to bag big game. Some hunters used mixed loads consisting of a scattering of shot on top of a lead ball when they were shooting fox or turkey.

The Kentucky's flintlock firing mechanism and the bullet mold had subsidiary uses. For example, one could start a fire by placing a tiny wad of unspun flax in the flashpan and sprinkling it with powder. When the trigger was pulled, sparks fell on the wad and started it burning. Then the wad was dropped into some tinder and a fire was lighted.

Bullet molds were made of brass, stone, or even from old curling irons. They resembled pliers, with a hollow in one jaw to shape the bullet. Anglers of the day used them also to cast weights for fishnets and seines.

Powder horns were carved with scenes, family histories, or maps. They were often scraped so thin that the black powder showed through, giving the hunter a constant check on his supply. The average horn was about eleven inches long and held up to three-quarters of a pound of powder. The priming-powder horn, which was carried in the pocket or in the hunting bag slung by a strap around the neck, was much smaller. The bag also contained a wire for cleaning the touchhole, flints, a few light tools, a bone needle for repairing ripped clothing, and extra bullets.

The early hunters preferred plain, open sights, which had a notch in the rear and a post or fin in front. Rear sights were placed on grooved slides, so horizontal adjustments were possible. Most frontiersmen sighted their rifles to shoot a bit high at fifty yards. The ball reached its peak height between fifty and a hundred yards, and at a hundred yards it registered a three-inch drop.

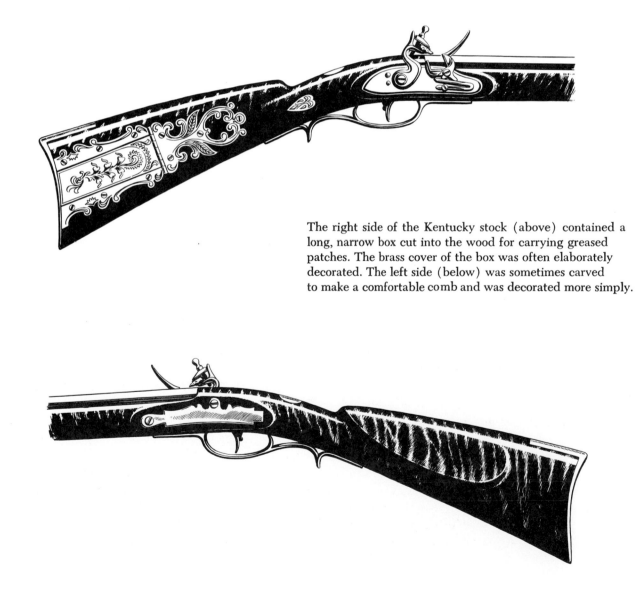

The right side of the Kentucky stock (above) contained a long, narrow box cut into the wood for carrying greased patches. The brass cover of the box was often elaborately decorated. The left side (below) was sometimes carved to make a comfortable comb and was decorated more simply.

Pinhead front sights, much like the modern bead sights, were standard for match shooting, and a wide variety of rear sights, including peep sights, were used. Some marksmen preferred a long brass or iron tube, about five-eighths of an inch in diameter and extending the full length of the barrel. Horizontal adjustments could be made because the sight was clamped to a sliding base at each end. A peephole in the eyecup and a pinhead front sight, fixed slightly below point-blank range, completed the setup. Users claimed they could get clearer definition of their targets. Some experts say that these were the sights Congress had in mind during the Revolution when it ordered the purchase of telescopes for use on rifles.

American pioneers who grew up with the Kentucky rifle in their hands were fine riflemen. As hunters they were silent and swift, and as target-shooters they were cool, self-confident, and accurate. And some of the womenfolk could match their husbands shot for shot. The wife of one gunsmith was acknowledged to be better than any rifleman in the area. It was her job to test each rifle made by her husband. Other women won their laurels the hard way—by clean hits on charging Indians. And many a self-reliant frontiersman, who balked at resting a rifle barrel on a

It took an accurate aim to "bark" a squirrel. Daniel Boone is said to have been one of the first masters at killing or stunning the bushy-tail by splintering bark under him.

prop for an ordinary shot, was glad to support it on his wife's shoulder to hit a difficult long-range target.

To judge wind velocity, these men watched the fluttering of the leaves. They knew many little tricks, including a few learned from the Indians and others handed down for several generations. One of these, the practice of stalking big game while hidden behind a horse, had been used by archers in Europe hundreds of years before. Another trick was to coax a bear from his hiding place in a big hollow log by sneaking up silently and tapping at intervals on the wood. Soon the beast would be so curious he would have to come out to investigate—just in time to be shot.

If his dog treed smaller game at night, the backwoodsman did not hesitate to climb the tree and shake the animal to the ground. If he wanted a change of diet, he could use his Kentucky rifle to shoot large fish. And to lure gobblers, he made a call with a turkey-wing bone.

Most owners of Kentucky rifles were so pleased with their fine weapons and so determined to improve their marksmanship that they practiced regularly and entered shooting contests of all kinds. In some turkey shoots, the birds were tied behind a bulletproof plank with only heads and necks showing. If the whole bird was in sight, the range was increased considerably.

Many shooting matches were held in the woods, with squirrels as targets. This was a natural form of competition, since most of the frontiersmen shot squirrels year in and year out and there were plenty of them. Using a Kentucky rifle, a modern Tennessee gunsmith, William Walker, is said to have shot forty squirrels without a miss in a match with a rival marksman.

From Kentucky-rifle days come picturesque stories about "barking" squirrels, a stunt which Daniel Boone is said to have been one of the first to perform. The purpose was to hit the bark of the tree directly under the squirrel. When this was done accurately, the bark splintered and the squirrel, killed or stunned by the concussion, was sent flying to the ground without a bullet hole in him.

George Washington learned the value of Kentucky riflemen during the French and Indians Wars. When the Revolution began, he urged the Continental Congress to put in a call for them. Most of the volunteers from the New England states and New York carried flintlock smoothbore muskets, and these were the guns issued to soldiers who did not bring their own sidearms. They were very good weapons, and many Americans were skilled in handling them, but they were still so inaccurate that nineteen shots out of twenty would miss on an eighteen-foot-square target at 350 yards. This performance was so poor that Benjamin Franklin suggested equipping the Continental Army with bows and arrows.

There were not enough Kentucky rifles to supply an army and no way to get them made quickly. But Washington knew that the sharpshooting riflemen could serve very special and useful purposes. At his insistence, the Congress resolved that "six companies of expert riflemen be immediately raised in Pennsylvania, two in Maryland, and two in Virginia . . . and march and join the Army near Boston." Within a month the men were on their way to Cambridge.

From the far fringes of the frontier the colorful, independent hunters flocked to their meeting places. One group of ninety-six men, recruited in Virginia by Daniel Morgan, marched six hundred miles in twenty-one days to join the army. And some of these rugged hunters had walked two hundred miles through the wilderness to enlist.

Like every other improvement in arms, from the longbow to the hydrogen bomb, the rifle was denounced as barbarous and uncivilized by the side that did not have it. After Bunker Hill, the British tried to explain their heavy losses by charging that the Americans used rifles with slit bullets that broke into four parts when fired. Actually, the frontier riflemen had not arrived at the time of the battle of Bunker Hill. Although the New England farmers who fought there were armed with muskets only, a writer of the time explained, "They are almost all marksmen, being accustomed to sporting of one kind or another from their youth." And they faced British soldiers armed with the same kind of weapon.

The men with the Kentuckys were marching northward, amazing townspeople with their marksmanship as well as their outlandish clothes and swaggering manners. The newspapers of the day were filled with stories of their feats—many of which obviously gained in the telling. From Lancaster, Pennsylvania, first home of the Kentucky, a townsman wrote of seeing a man take a five-by-seven-inch piece of board and hold it between his knees while, from a distance of sixty yards, his brother put eight bullets through it in succession. Another man offered to shoot an apple off a man's head at the same range, but the timid spectators declined to watch such a harrowing performance.

After they joined the army at Cambridge,

To lure a bear from a hollow log, the hunter would tap on the wood until the bruin came out to investigate.

the backwoodsmen made life miserable for the British. Their specialty was picking off officers and sentries. Soon a Philadelphia printer was writing to a friend in London, "This province has raised 1,000 riflemen, the worst of whom will put a ball into a man's head at the distance of 150 or 200 yards. Therefore advise your officers who shall hereafter come out to America to settle their affairs in England before their departure." Some Britishers called the Kentuckys "the most fatal widow and orphan makers in the world."

British General Howe is said to have offered a large reward for the capture of a Kentucky rifleman. When one was finally taken, Howe sent him to London to show what the redcoats were facing. A few demonstrations of his skill slowed British enlistments considerably.

The riflemen may occasionally have overdone their long-range shooting. Some American officers felt that by attempting too many "preposterous" shots the backwoodsmen were wasting ammunition and getting so many misses that they might lessen the wholesome respect the British had for them. Consequently some units were given strict orders not to fire at any target more than 150 yards away.

The shot that may have won independence was fired by Daniel Murphy, a frontiersman with General Dan Morgan's outfit. At a critical moment in the Battle of Saratoga, Murphy was ordered to pick off the British General Fraser, a highly competent officer who was trying to rally the redcoats and seemed to be succeeding. Fraser was standing with two aides on a hill about 300 yards from Murphy's position. The backwoodsman loaded, sighted his long-barreled Kentucky rifle, and fired. One of the aides fell. Murphy loaded, fired again, and missed. By this time Fraser knew he was being shot at, but his code of honor and his determination to rally his forces forced him to stay where he was. And he could not believe that anyone could hit him at such a distance. At the third shot, he fell dead. His men turned and fled, and the tide of battle

was turned. With the American victory over General Burgoyne, the British effort to split the colonies in two failed. Moreover, France was so impressed by the victory that it finally decided to give substantial aid to the colonies.

Just how good was the Kentucky rifle? Fortunately, its worth need not be determined from legendary accounts. Modern firearms collectors have actually tried out the old flintlocks in hunting and target work, and have tested their ballistics by scientific methods.

The results of one of these tests were reported by Townsend Whelen in his book, *The American Rifle*. The gun was a Rosser flintlock made in Lancaster, Pennsylvania, in 1739. It fired a round ball with a .32-inch diameter, a weight of 49 grains, and a charge of 22 grains of black powder. The test was made at the Remington—Union Metallic Cartridge Company factory, and here are the figures:

Muzzle velocity ....1,483 foot seconds
Muzzle energy ....239 foot pounds
Velocity at 100 yards ....850 foot seconds
Energy at 100 yards ....79 foot pounds
Velocity at 200 yards ....617 foot seconds
Energy at 200 yards ....41 foot pounds

According to Whelen, the best range for rifles of this type was about 60 yards. They were seldom used, he says, at more than a 100 yards, and beyond 150 yards they were not reliable. In power, he classed them with the relatively modern .25 Stevens rimfire cartridge at short ranges.

A more flattering picture was given in hunting and target tests made by Captain John G. W. Dillin, collector and authority on Kentucky rifles. In 1921 Dillin took a famous flintlock called "Old Killdeer" to a farm and had "a well-known offhand rifleman" try it out. The first targets were pigeons sitting on a high barn, thirty to thirty-five yards away. Two birds were killed in three shots. The rifleman even called his shots—"High up, as I aimed above the center of the body." On the same trip, three starlings and a sparrow were hit at fifteen to forty yards—a total of six dead birds for eight shots, strictly offhand.

On another occasion, Dillin took "a good flintlock" to Ontario and tried it on wild ducks. Out of three shots at ducks swimming 150 yards away, he hit one bird squarely through the body and another in the wing. The miss was the first shot and resulted from overestimating the drop of the bullet.

With Walter M. Cline of Tennessee, Dillin tested three Kentucky rifles (a spiral-groove, a straight-cut, and a smoothbore) on standard silhouette targets that were the size of an average man. Out of ten shots each at three hundred yards, the spiral scored five hits, the straight-cut two, and the smoothbore one. Beyond three hundred yards, Dillin reported, the percentage of hits was very small.

While these cold figures tend to shrink some of the taller stories of frontier legend, the fact remains that the Kentucky rifle, compared with other sporting and military arms of the time, represented a revolutionary improvement in firearms and was a truly great weapon, worthy of the men who used it.

CHAPTER 7

The Birth of Modern Firearms

For almost a hundred years the American frontiersman believed he had the perfect weapon in the Kentucky rifle. It was so much better than anything that had come before that he felt it could never be improved. Then some of those frontiersmen began to move westward from the forest regions over the Great Plains and into the Rockies. They took their Kentuckys with them, of course, but they were not the perfect weapons for these new environments. The Kentucky was still an excellent firearm for the relatively light game they had known, the whitetail deer and the black bear, but it had been bred a little too fine for the big Western animals.

In the first place, it was not a saddle rifle, and men took to horses when they traversed the Plains. A weapon fifty-one to seventy-seven inches long was just too unwieldy for a man on a horse. Secondly, it did not have enough shocking power to stop a tough buffalo or huge grizzlies. As a result of these practical discoveries, a new weapon emerged, the "Plains rifle," made famous by Hawken and other gunmakers. Ball caliber, which had been as small as .32 in the Kentucky, went up to .50 and larger. The length of rifle barrels was cut to thirty inches. The Plains rifle was a saddle weapon of relatively short range and heavy shocking power. It filled an important need for a few years, but actually was not an important step in the development of firearms. It was a kind of reversion, in fact, to the old European Jaeger rifle.

Other and much more lasting improvements were on the way, notably breech-loading and percussion firing. Around 1800, the United States began fifty years of experimentation with firearms that were to bring them to the threshold of modern design.

Every American, hunter or not, has heard the story of how the rifle helped win the West. Not so many know how important it was in the growth of American industry. Interchangeable parts, mass production, the assembly line—all innovations that helped make us a great industrial nation—were initiated by firearms manufacturers. And the demands of these men for better and more steel spurred research. Crucible steel had become available in the mid-seventeen hundreds. During the eighteen thirties blast furnaces were improved; in the eighteen fifties came the Bessemer process, and a decade later the perfection of the open-hearth process. With better steel, gun barrels could be produced that were stronger and lighter.

The hunter, however, was not thinking about such technical and long-range matters in the early eighteen hundreds. He was looking for a better gun. The flintlock firing mechanism, for example, was not invariably dependable, no matter how much better it was than its predecessors. The priming powder was still susceptible to damp weather, or might fail to ignite for other reasons. Hunters and frontiersmen were beginning to hope for a sure-fire method of ignition.

And muzzle-loading a rifle was still difficult and time consuming, as it had been for centuries. With the Kentucky, a man shooting from cover had to get to his feet, pour powder down the barrel, patch a ball, and ram it home. By that time a fleeing whitetail could be half a mile away. But with a good breechloader, he would scarcely have to change position to send off another shot quickly.

There was a third need, only dimly felt at the time but nevertheless important. Today we would call it a repair-service system. In those days every rifle was a handmade product of a gunmaker, and no two were exactly alike. When a hunter broke one part he had to have a new one fashioned by hand, and that took more time than he liked.

Many men in different countries had been trying to find the answer to these three problems for years. Curiously, the first practical solutions came almost at the same time. In 1798 Eli Whitney conceived the idea and demonstrated the practicability of interchangeable parts. In 1807 a Scottish preacher, Alexander J. Forsyth, patented the first per-

To sell his idea of interchangeable parts, Eli Whitney scrambled the pieces of six muskets and reassembled them before an Army ordnance board.

cussion system for firearms. And in 1811 an American, Captain John H. Hall, developed the first accurate breechloader. It took some time for all these improvements to be combined in a single weapon, but it was inevitable that they would.

Eli Whitney was a Yankee genius who invented the cotton gin in 1793. When his reward turned out to be very little money and a series of lawsuits for patent infringement, he turned in disgust to the manufacture of firearms, although at the time he knew little about guns. He had something more important, however, than a specific knowledge about any one product—the concept of uniformity, precision, and a manufacturing procedure that would lead to mass production. He broke with the traditional methods of manufacturing guns—and everything else. Firearms had been made by the individual gunsmith, who made the whole weapon from start to finish, fashioning and fitting its parts as he went along. These were good guns when made by a good smith, but each part was a little different from the same part on any other gun.

Eli Whitney took one good musket, dismantled it completely, and had his workmen duplicate its parts exactly. When he had half a dozen muskets made by this method, he took them and two of his mechanics before an Army ordnance board—according to some accounts. The workmen took the guns apart, mixed the parts up thoroughly on the floor, and then reassembled six muskets from parts picked at random. Each of the reassembled weapons worked perfectly. Impressed, the Army gave Whitney a contract to manufacture ten thousand muskets—a big order for those days. But Eli Whitney had more than an order; he had one of the basic ideas on which modern industry is based.

The man who supplied the answer to the second big question about gun development in the eighteen hundreds was more of a firearms expert than Whitney was. The Scottish preacher, Alexander J. Forsyth, began experimenting with materials for percussion firing in the seventeen nineties and was granted a patent in 1807. It had long been known that certain metallic chemicals—salts of fulminic acid—would explode violently under a smart blow. To make a fulminate—of mercury in most cases, although silver and other metals were also used—the experimenter would dissolve one part of mercury in ten parts of nitric acid, then pour the solution into alcohol. A furious reaction followed, and eventually the salt, or fulminate, settled to the bottom of the flask in the form of crystals.

Although the properties of fulminates had been known for some time, apparently no one before Forsyth connected them with firearms. His method of applying them to a gun was crude but simple. First, he tapped the flash hole of a musket and inserted a small, hollow plug. Then he attached a rather clumsy gadget which served both as a magazine for the fulminate of mercury and as a striker to set it off. The hollow magazine end of the device held twenty charges of the fulminate. After the shooter had loaded his musket with powder and ball through the muzzle, he tilted the magazine so that a measured amount of the fulminate fell into the hollow plug. Then he reversed the device, bringing the cocked striker into place. When he pulled the trigger, the hammer fell on the plug and exploded the fulminate, which sent sparks through the flash hole and ignited the main charge.

The Forsyth primer was really no more dependable than the flintlock, for rain could put it out of commission. And it was dangerous. Fulminate of mercury is a very unstable substance, likely to blow up if jarred too roughly. Sometimes that jar came when the hammer flew back, or when the shooter dropped his musket or knocked it against a tree. Then the magazine blew apart.

The Maynard tapelock was the action used on this
U.S. Army rifle Model 1855. The Army paid Dr. Maynard
$75,000 for the military rights to his lock.

In spite of these drawbacks, which concerned only the practical application of his basic idea, Forsyth deserves credit for one of the greatest forward steps in firearms history. Scores of tinkerers set to work at once to improve the application of his principles. Most of them sought easier and safer ways of feeding the loose fulminate crystals into the flash plug, and failed. In 1814, however, a Philadelphia artist, Joshua Shaw, invented a device that made the percussion system practical. It was the primer cap. His first cap was made of iron, being intended for repeated use, but it did not work well. So he switched to copper, and from that time the percussion system was on its way.

Shaw's cap looked like a miniature of the stovepipe hat of his day. Into the open end he poured fulminate of mercury, which he sealed in place with a foil disk. The cap was made to fit over a channeled nipple which had been inserted in the flash hole of a musket. When the shooter had loaded his gun with powder and ball, he placed the cap on the nipple, aimed, and pulled the trigger. Since the cap was not affected by dampness, the mechanism rarely malfunctioned.

Many hunters began using the Shaw cap immediately, although some old-timers derided it as unnecessary and dangerous. The Army, which had money to finance inventors, played safe by paying for research in percussion and sticking to the flintlock in production. Some inventors tried to improve on Shaw's cap by devising an automatic cap-priming system. One led a tiny copper tube containing the fulminate up to the flash plug, where the falling hammer pinched off a portion and fired it. Another cut similar tubing into small sections in advance and fed them into the plug one by one. But none of these methods was dependable to any great extent; consequently new ones were developed.

The field of firearms development was beginning to attract more and more people, but some of the non-experts contributed the most important inventions. We have seen how a preacher and an artist played significant roles in percussion development. Next came a dentist, Dr. Edward Maynard, of Washington, D.C. Dr. Maynard took two narrow strips of varnished paper, placed fulminate of mercury "pills" at regular intervals between them, then sealed the strips together and wound them into a coil. His product, which came to be known as the Maynard tapelock, was remarkably like the rolls of paper caps for cap pistols that children use today.

The dentist designed an action to feed his tape into the flash plug. It consisted of a compartment to hold the coil of pills and a spring device which moved the caps upward when the trigger was pulled. There was always a fresh cap in place, the used one having been clipped off by the falling hammer.

Actually, the Maynard tapelock was not an important step in the development of firearms, but rather an ingenious and quite successful side excursion. The lock worked well in dry weather, but the paper could not be waterproofed enough to protect the fulminate in damp weather. However, the tape took the fancy of many hunters, who had their flintlocks converted to the new system.

The Army not only paid Dr. Maynard $75,000—a fortune in 1845—for the military rights to his lock, but also gave him a contract to produce rifles. Just as he was getting into production, however, his factory burned down. He managed to get another factory going, but no large quantities of his rifles were produced for military use. When the Civil War ended, the tape was becoming obsolete, but

Maynard had a number of actions on hand and built them into sporting rifles.

In the half-century before the Civil War there were many improvements in the rifle through extensive experimentation. But since there were no big firearms companies to finance research and encourage inventors, most advances were made independently. The Army was not sure of its goals; military leaders, for example, were for a long time uninterested in rapid fire, contending that it merely gave the soldier a chance to waste more ammunition. Though skeptical of radical change, the Army did provide financial aid and jobs for some of the more practical firearms inventors. Among these was John H. Hall, designer of one of the first practical breechloaders.

Hall patented his device in 1811. It was, in effect, a two-section barrel, the front part being like the ordinary barrel of the day except that it was open at both ends. The short rear section, a rectangular block of iron, was lined up with the barrel when locked in place. But it was pivoted at the rear so it could be swung up, presenting a chamber about an inch deep. Into this chamber the riflemen poured 100 grains of black powder, then pressed in by hand a .525-caliber bullet that weighed 219 grains. The ball was slightly larger than the barrel bore, so that it would engage the rifling firmly without a patch. With a ball and

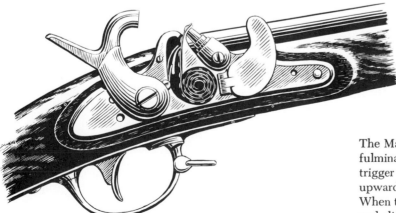

The Maynard percussion tapelock used "pills" of fulminate sealed in a roll of paper tape. When the trigger was pulled, a spring action moved the tape upward and into position over the flash plug. When the hammer fell, it exploded the fulminate and clipped off the used tape.

The Hall breechloader had a rectangular section at the rear of the barrel which pivoted up, exposing an inch-deep chamber to take the powder and ball. When the breech section was snapped down into position, the chamber was aligned with the barrel ready for firing.

powder in place, the shooter pushed the chamber block back into line with the barrel and locked it. Then he was ready to fire. The first Hall rifle used a flintlock firing mechanism, but later models were adapted to percussion.

Compared with rifles that were to follow, such as the Sharps, the Hall was awkward to handle, but it was a great improvement over the ramrod-and-patch method of the Kentucky. The Hall was not a pleasant gun to shoot, because a fair amount of gas escaped through the imperfect joining of the barrel and the chamber block. Nevertheless, it propelled its .525 bullet at about 1,400 foot seconds, while the Kentucky mustered about 1,500 to 1,600 foot seconds. Muzzle energy of the Hall was about 1,500 foot seconds. The gun's overall length was fifty-two and a half inches.

The Hall was, of course, not nearly as easy to reload as a modern single-shot rifle, but it was much faster than any muzzle-loader. A hunter had a reasonably good chance to get off a second shot quickly if his first one missed, especially since he didn't have to get to his feet and reveal himself to his game. Moreover, the Hall rifle was dependable and accurate. The oversize ball not only gripped the rifling firmly but kept the barrel fairly clean, thus helping to prevent the fluctuations in muzzle energy which affect accuracy.

The hunter of those days needed all the accuracy he could get, despite the amount of game available. The Kentucky was a good rifle in the right hands but, as we have seen, some of the old legends about it must be heard with a bit of skepticism. Still, it rarely failed for the man who had learned how to use it carefully; he knew his rifle, kept it clean as a whistle, measured his powder precisely, and judged windage with uncanny accuracy. Even then, he was no better than the rifle he carried. And the rifle was no better than its black powder and round lead balls, whether it was muzzle-loader or breechloader.

The Army made some tests of rifles during the early eighteen hundreds, firing round balls from a rest. When a long string was fired at an eight-by-eight-foot target, ninety-five per cent of the balls hit the target at two hundred yards. At three hundred yards only sixty-five per cent got on, and at four hundred yards only thirty-five per cent. This was the best shooting of a number of tests, and gives a good idea of what the hunter of those days had to face. Moreover, the rifles had to be aimed for an exceedingly high trajectory. With the rifle sighted for two hundred yards, its ball rose 14.5 inches above the line of sight at fifty yards, 18.8 inches at seventy-five yards, and 19.7 inches at a hundred yards. If the hunter was not an expert judge of distance, the odds were pitted heavily against him even before he lined up his sights.

These shortcomings were found in the breechloader as well as the muzzle-loader, although the oversize ball of the breech gun usually got a better spin and a bit more stable flight. Even then, a sudden, strong gust of wind would take the round ball off its course. Wind continued to bother all shooters until the conical, or elongated, bullet came along about the time of the Civil War. When a round ball was used, the wind could easily cause the best marksman to miss, and if the target happened to be a deer, the beast was probably far away before the hunter could shoot again, even with the Hall.

Not all game was as fast and wary as the whitetail. When the United States was young, the wapiti, or American elk, roamed over the entire continent, including the Eastern seaboard. (It was not until the mid-eighteen hundreds that these creatures became extinct in such states as Pennsylvania and Kentucky.) But the elk was not very bright; it seemed to have little or no instinct for self-preservation. When wagon trains passed through wapiti country, it was not at all unusual for a bull to lope along with one for hours, often no more than a hundred yards away. Occasionally, the old hunters reported, he would sound a weak

sort of challenge. If there was plenty of meat in the wagons, he had a fifty-fifty chance of surviving. Not many emigrants wanted to add excess weight to their wagons or waste a valuable lead ball.

More often, however, the elk's curiosity was his undoing. Many a hunter or explorer, cooking a lonely meal over a campfire, was startled to see a big bull elk stalk out of the forest to look at him. A casual reach for the rifle, a shot, and the hunter had fresh liver for his pan. Who cared if the rest of the magnificent animal was left to rot? Before steps were taken to save the elk from extinction not many years ago, some men shot them just to get their teeth. They made attractive watch charms.

The wapiti's stupidity almost doomed him. A century ago it was possible for two riflemen to destroy an entire herd without taking more than a few steps. The elk just milled around aimlessly as one after another was shot down. Most American hunters did not get such easy shooting, however, so they required an accurate gun that could make the most of the first shot. The Hall, more than any rifle before it, supplied that accuracy.

More important, it helped revolutionize rifle manufacture and paved the way for the Sharps, Ballards, Henrys, Winchesters, and Remingtons that were to come. For John Hall was a disciple of Eli Whitney, a firm believer in the importance of interchangeable parts, and he found himself in a position to further that significant manufacturing concept.

When the Army gave Hall's breechloaders some exhaustive tests in direct competition with a standard muzzle-loader, the Hall proved to be superior in every way. The military authorities decided that, although the muzzle-loader would probably remain the standard weapon, it would be a good idea to have some breechloaders on hand. So Captain Hall was appointed as assistant armorer at Harpers Ferry Arsenal and given the job of producing his own rifles for the government.

He spent $60,000 on machine tools and went to work. Between 1819 and 1825 he produced Hall rifles at a cost of $21.57 each; by 1835 he had brought the cost down to $14.50.

Hall was a fanatic about interchangeable parts and mass production, and would allow no interference with his methods. Once he heard that a contractor who had been given an order for Hall rifles planned to make some changes and "improvements." Hall made a long and spirited protest. He told officials that interchangeability not only cut original costs, speeded production, and made repairs simple, but saved the government large sums of money, since the parts of damaged weapons could be salvaged and used again. He insisted that there must be no tendency to make small changes here and there. The parts of a Hall

rifle made at Harpers Ferry should be interchangeable with the parts of a Hall made anywhere else.

Hall's subordinates at the arsenal were inspired by his ideas. But at least one of them realized that although the Hall methods were admirable, the Hall rifle was certainly less than perfect. The old story was about to be repeated. For decades men had thought the Kentucky a perfect rifle, one that could not be improved. Then came the Hall rifle, but already one of Hall's own workers began to think of improvements he could make. He was Christian Sharps. The guns he later designed and manufactured were prized by hunters, distinguished themselves above all others in the Civil War, and were a decisive factor in the long war against the grizzly in the West.

The Hall breechloader gave the hunter a chance to reload and fire a second shot without exposing himself to the game.

CHAPTER 8

When the Grizzly Ruled the West

The grizzly bear of the West, bearing the appropriate scientific name of *Ursus horribilis,* was so different from the smaller black bear of the Eastern forests that they might have been totally different genera. The Eastern black bear was, on occasion, quite playful; and he was the "coward" to whom the Indian apologized before hitting him over the head with a club.

But the grizzly was no coward, in anyone's view, and the Indians of his territory kept out of his way or hunted him with great respect and caution. According to the men who conquered the West, the grizzly was the toughest and most courageous foe ever to face the hunters of this country. Today you have to travel many miles to find him, but he is still the cantankerous, unpredictable monster he was a hundred years ago—more wary now, more knowing about the ways of man, but still ready to fight anyone who pushes him too hard.

There is nothing debatable about the big bear's savagery, although there are many who insist that a grizzly will not attack a man without provocation. But as one old-timer, a veteran of battles against the beasts, said, "After all, it is the bear that decides what provocation is; sometimes you just have to be in

the same county with him to get him riled."

The grizzly has dealt an agonizing death to a great number of men, and an even greater number have escaped badly slashed and beaten. The big bear has the ability—and when aroused, the desire—to maul a man to death, or tear him to ribbons with his fangs and claws. A few grizzlies still roam the Rockies, chiefly in Montana and Wyoming, but in the main they have vanished from the West they once dominated. But in the mountains of western Canada, and in Alaska and the subarctic, grizzlies and their close relatives, the big brown Alaska bears, are still the reigning monarchs of the range.

Nowadays, of course, the modern hunter has the upper hand in a contest with a grizzly. Modern rifles and ammunition, properly selected and handled, have the shocking power of a bolt of lightning. And, if necessary, the hunter can get off a second or third shot while the echo of the first is still ringing. Even so, he may be in difficulty. The grizzly can absorb an unbelievable amount of lead and keep on coming. At such a time a wrong move or a touch of panic can be fatal.

An example of the grizzly's ability to take punishment and keep on fighting was given by a group of early explorers in the West. In one encounter, eight of the men shot at a grizzly, each putting a bullet into his body. Instead of collapsing, the bear took out after the hunters with considerable vigor, chasing them all into a river and plunging in after them. He was gaining rapidly on two of the swimmers when another hunter came running along the bank. He fired a single shot, which struck the tenacious animal in the brain and killed him instantly.

Obviously, the weapons brought by the first explorers and hunters were not adequate for the job they had to do against the grizzly. And encountering one was not a rare event in those days. There were so many of them a century and a quarter ago—a rider might spot fifteen or twenty in one day—that they were a major obstacle to the development of the

West, and until about 1860 men did not have guns good enough to kill grizzlies.

The first men to seek their fortunes in the West had little choice of the firearms they would carry. Around 1800, the Kentucky was about the best all-around rifle a man could buy, but it had been designed for the lighter game of the East. With its .45- or .50-caliber and low muzzle velocity, a grizzly hunter had to get in close if he hoped to make a kill—and he had to make a head or heart shot. A hit anywhere else merely enraged the bear, causing him to charge at once with speed and determination to kill.

The muzzle-loading hunter rarely got a chance for a second shot unless he took it from a tree. Even the most expert hunter needed time to pour a charge of black powder down the barrel, then patch and ram home a bullet. When he was deer-hunting, the loading time

Meriwether Lewis, of the Lewis and Clark expedition, had a close call with a silvertip when it caught him with his rifle unloaded after killing a buffalo.

meant that he would probably lose his quarry. But when he was hunting grizzlies it could easily mean death. The prudent hunter who missed or merely wounded on his first shot scrambled up the nearest tree and was grateful for one great difference between the grizzly and the black bear of the East—the grizzly could not climb.

The story of the Western grizzly might be called "The Hundred Years' War." Before 1810 he was almost unknown; after 1910 he was practically extinct. The Spanish settlers in California had, to their sorrow, been aware of him from the time they first came there in the latter half of the sixteenth century. The big beast had no respect for their vineyards, orchards, or livestock—and almost none for the Spaniards themselves. He was a particularly vicious terror with sheep. Even the fire barriers that some shepherds built around their flocks failed to keep him away. He would find a gap somewhere, plunge through, and maul ten or twelve sheep to death while the shepherds cringed in terror. When the situation became too bad in a particular region, the authorities would call in the militia. In the face of twenty or thirty smoothbores, even the toughest grizzly did not have much chance. But the soldiers made no appreciable dent in the bear population; this was a job that would have required an entire army to range through the forests on constant alert.

Easterners learned something of the grizzly when the explorers Lewis and Clark brought back word of him. Meriwether Lewis and William Clark were two frontiersmen-soldiers who had served with distinction in the Revolution. In 1804 they were selected by President Thomas Jefferson as leaders of the first great exploring expedition into the vast Western lands acquired through the Louisiana Purchase the year before. Starting from the junction of the Mississippi and Missouri, they worked their way up the latter, then through the Yellowstone country and into the Pacific Northwest. Accompanying them were forty-three experienced hunters and woodsmen.

The journals of the expedition do not state just where the men first encountered grizzlies. "Big bears" are mentioned but are described merely as "brown," "white," or "yellow." Apparently the explorers thought these were distinct species, which is not surprising in view of the fact that the grizzly does come in a wide range of colors. But when Lewis and Clark reached the Yellowstone they found the "typical" Western grizzly and gave a good description of it. The name "grizzly" began to be used more and more frequently in referring to the huge Western bears.

Naturalists now distinguish eighty-odd forms of the grizzly and the closely allied Alaska brown bear. In the early eighteen hundreds they ranged from northern Mexico up through Canada to Alaska and the subarctic. In what is now the United States, grizzlies were everywhere in the vast territory that was to be divided later into California, Nevada, Wyoming, Oregon, Washington, Utah, Montana, Idaho, and the Dakotas. There were also some in the Texas mountains, western Nebraska, and northwestern Kansas.

The coat of most grizzlies was dark brown, deepening to black along the spine and on the legs and ears with a white patch behind each shoulder. The fur was tipped with white, which gave the bear his nickname, silvertip. But some bears—especially those in California—had little tipping; their coats were dark brown or cocoa-color. Other had so much tipping that they seemed to be wearing dirty polar-bear coats. Still others ran to various shades of yellow.

Like many later hunters, members of the Lewis and Clark expedition apparently overestimated the size and weight of the grizzlies they saw. There seems to be some quality about a live silvertip that makes him look larger and heavier than he is. For example, a famous naturalist tells of observing a "monster" grizzly one day in the Rockies. He estimated it to be at least four feet high at the shoulder when walking on all fours, which would have made it a big bear indeed. But he found a means of checking his estimate, because the silvertip walked under a low-hanging branch. Later the naturalist measured the distance from the ground to the branch and found it to be exactly thirty-six inches.

Almost every hunter who killed a grizzly in the old days estimated it to weigh at least a thousand pounds. Actually, the typical grizzly probably weighed around five hundred pounds. One famous hunter, Colonel W. D. Pickett of Wyoming, killed forty grizzlies in thirty-five years, and the largest weighed exactly eight hundred pounds.

The Lewis and Clark hunters, assuming at first that the grizzly had the same characteristics as the smaller, rather timid black bear of the East, made the mistake of getting tough with the big beast. This attitude did not last long, however. As Lewis wrote in his journal, their "curiosity" about the grizzly was soon "well satisfied," a gem of understatement. On the contrary many of the early hunters wished the grizzly had never been created, for he pushed them off the trail, chased them up trees or into rivers, and generally made their lives dangerous and difficult.

As settlers moved westward in the decades following the Lewis and Clark expedition, they found the grizzly a continual menace to themselves and to their livestock. The silvertip by nature is not inclined to stray far from a location in which the forage is good. And he soon made it clear that he would not move out just because man had decided to move in. In fact, the arrival of livestock gave him a good reason to stay right where he was.

The farmers and cattlemen did their best to exterminate the bear, using traps and poison as well as rifles. But there were too many grizzlies and not enough hunters. Although the grizzly was essentially a mountain bear, he got along well in the foothills and adjacent plains. He would eat anything—grass, leaves, bark, roots, berries, nuts, honey, insects, frogs, snakes, fish, eggs, birds—and any animal from a mouse to a moose. It should be noted that some grizzlies were not killers in that they showed little interest in meat if other food was at hand. But most of them liked meat, and all would go and get it when they needed it. A grizzly might skirt a buffalo herd, scavenging on dead animals. Occasionally he might manage to kill a cow or a calf, or an old bull. The young bulls were too fast for him to catch.

Domestic livestock was easy prey. Usually the grizzly would grab a heifer, but he would take a full-grown steer if it was handy. Some ranches reported that steers were felled and dragged half a mile. And the bears were impudent about the whole business, showing a readiness to take on any rancher who interfered.

One cattleman told about finding a freshly killed steer, so he took his rifle and climbed a tree to await the return of the bear. However, it was dark when the bear came back for his dinner, and the rancher could not shoot. The grizzly scented the man at once and forgot all about his food. He searched the area carefully, then methodically beat down every clump of brush for an acre around, obviously hoping to flush his antagonist. He never located the man, but the rancher spent a long and uncomfortable evening on his perch.

Can a man fight a grizzly hand-to-hand and live to tell the tale? Many thrilling yarns of this kind have come out of the West. A favorite form of barroom art was the gaudy lithograph showing a hardy hunter, armed only with his trusty knife, locked in deadly combat with a grizzly. Even in our own time, some men have taken on grizzlies in this fashion—always from necessity. Some lived to tell the tale. Some did not.

Many a hard-pressed hunter was forced to climb a tree—thankful to use the bear's inability to climb to good advantage.

A hunter preferred to tackle the grizzly armed with a good rifle. The Kentucky proved too weak and too long. The plains rifle was little better, although a mounted man could handle it fairly well. One of the favorite guns to be brought into the West was the "Harpers Ferry" rifle, a muzzle-loader made by Remington which had become the principle infantry weapon of the Union Army in the Civil War. This percussion-action gun was said to have such accuracy that a good marksman could hit a deer at six hundred yards with it, and at one thousands yards the bullets retained enough power to penetrate five inches of pine—or to kill a grizzly with a well-placed shot.

The Hall breechloader, described in the last chapter, was a definite improvement over the muzzle-loaders because of its faster action. But an even bigger step forward came with the Sharps rifle. Christian Sharps, a fine technician, worked under Hall at Harpers Ferry from 1830 to 1844, at which time he had enough good ideas to start on his own. In 1848, he obtained his basic patent on a rifle of really revolutionary design. Its principle feature was the sliding breechblock, which not only was much stronger and safer than Hall's but permitted quick and easy loading. The rifle was chambered for a cartridge, rather than loose powder and ball, and shot one of the early elongated bullets.

The block, operated by a lever which also served as a trigger guard, slid up and down in a strong metal frame. When the lever was pushed forward, the block was depressed, exposing the chamber in the barrel breech. The rifleman placed his cartridge—the first kind was a paper tube containing bullet and powder—in the chamber and pulled back the lever. The ascending block sheared off the cartridge's paper tail, exposing the powder for the percussion flash. A number of percussion systems were used on the Sharps, including the Maynard tapelock, Sharps's own automatic pellet primer, and the individual copper cap. Early Sharps models employed an external hammer to explode the percussion cap, but later guns had an internal firing pin and chambered the metallic cartridge.

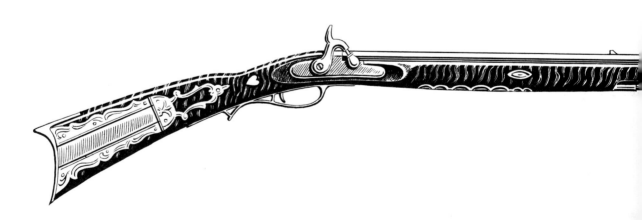

The new rifle and the other famous guns that were to follow it in short order meant the eventual end of the grizzly menace. Although the Sharps was a single-shot arm, a good rifleman could get off nine or more shots a minute with it. A heavy powder charge gave the .54-caliber, 475-grain bullet excellent striking power and considerable accuracy.

The Army was slow to adopt the Sharps rifle. Many staff men preferred careful aiming to rapidity of fire. But within a few years, the Civil War was to decide the issue in favor of the breechloader. Meanwhile, in the decade before the war, hunters welcomed the Sharps enthusiastically. From 1850 to 1855 they bought almost fourteen thousand rifles, and by 1860 the Sharps factory was making them at the rate of thirty thousand a year.

Soon after its introduction, the Sharps rifle became a factor in the sectional differences that led to the Civil War. During the eighteen fifties, New England abolitionists sent many emigrants to border areas in the hope of gaining the power to insure that new states, such as Kansas, would not have slavery. For "protection" they armed the settlers with Sharps rifles; in 1855–56 almost a thousand were bought for that purpose. The rifle also attained some fame when the famous Northern preacher, Henry Ward Beecher, declared it to be more valuable than the Bible in settling intersectional strife. Sharps rifles soon became know as "Beecher's Bibles."

The abolitionists often shipped them to the Kansas Territory in boxes marked "Bibles." Once, word came to the pro-South faction that a hundred Sharps carbines were being shipped on a Missouri River steamer. When the vessel docked at Lexington, Missouri, a mob boarded it and seized the firearms. But when they broke open the cases, they howled with rage and disappointment. The canny New Englanders had removed all the breechblocks and shipped them by a different route.

A few years later, John Brown talked the abolitionists into giving him two hundred Sharps carbines for "safekeeping." Thus armed, he proceeded with his fantastic plan to seize the Harpers Ferry arsenal, arm the slaves, and sweep through the South. The insurrection was quickly put down by Federal

Many Kentucky rifles were converted to percussion systems employing an external hammer to explode the percussion cap. But even with "modernized" firing, the Kentucky didn't have the stopping power needed for grizzlies.

troops under the command of Colonel Robert E. Lee. The confiscated Sharps were stored at the arsenal. Eventually those guns—bought by abolitionists—were recaptured by the Confederacy and used to arm some of its cavalry.

The part that the Sharps played in the Civil War need not be discussed here, except to say that it gained tremendous prestige on both sides. When the war was over a large number of the rifles, both military and hunting models, were carried into the West. There, in time, they gained their greatest fame in the hands of the buffalo hunters, as we shall see in Chapter Nine. But they also proved effective against the terrible grizzly. And they became even more potent when new models, chambering the metallic cartridge, began to pour out of the Sharps factories.

The Sharps and other single-shot rifles passed sentence on the grizzly, but the repeater finally carried out the execution. In the years following the Civil War, one great rifle after another appeared. The grizzly was doomed, but he fought long and hard. As one California writer put it just before the turn of the century, "Each year the hunters kill large numbers of bears, and each year the bears kill a considerable number of hunters."

Some Westerners hunted in groups, running the grizzlies down with dogs and then shooting them. Gradually the bears were driven up into the mountains, but many of them continued their raiding. Some became so shrewd that they were never caught. One big grizzly was reported to have killed nearly a thousand sheep in fifteen years. A large reward spurred the search for him, but despite the use of dogs, traps, and poison, he was never taken. He would sneak down out of the hills every two or three days, kill a sheep, and then disappear. During the entire fifteen years, he was seen only two or three times.

This grizzly was just one of a dwindling number of survivors. In the closing decades of the nineteenth century, *Ursus horribilis* became more and more scarce. Sportsmen who went west to hunt the grizzly after 1910 found him a rare and elusive animal—and a far greater prize for that very reason. They sought him as a worthy trophy, not something to slaughter as an obstacle to progress.

CHAPTER 9

The Slaughter of the Buffalo

The world has probably never known a wild four-legged animal that bred in such astounding numbers as the buffalo (or bison, to give its correct name). Its population on the North American continent before the coming of the white man reached the tremendous figure of seventy-five million, according to the most conservative estimates (to two hundred million, according to the highest). The shocking fact in connection with this great animal is that by 1890 there were only a few hundred left.

The unprecedented slaughter began soon after the white man first came to these shores, although it did not reach its peak for another three hundred years. The Indians had been hunting the buffalo for centuries, but they were never greedy or really wasteful, and their bows and arrows had little effect on the buffalo population. Even after they obtained guns and horses, the Indians could not possibly have wiped out the hordes of buffalo that existed.

The first European to see a buffalo came upon it in a menagerie. The man was Cortes, the Spanish conqueror of Mexico, and the menagerie was one that had been assembled by the Aztec emperor Montezuma. The Spaniards were amazed at this new type of "cow."

One of them wrote learnedly that it was a "composite of several and divers animals," since it had the lion's mane, flanks, and tufted tail; the goat's beard; the camel's hump; and the cow's hoofs.

The Spaniards were even more astounded when they saw the buffalo in its natural habitat. Never had they come upon such an enormous concentration of animals. One little band of explorers made a dramatic report of an encounter with bison. They were first attracted by a peculiar reddish haze beyond a range of low hills. Climbing a hill to investigate, they saw a vast "brown sea" of beasts, a restless, moving mass of animals that stretched as far as the eye could see. They were buffaloes —hundreds of thousands of them. But that was only the beginning. The explorers pushed on for weeks and never lost sight of the animals, who no doubt numbered several million in that single huge herd. The explorers sent glowing accounts back to Spain, declaring the new "cattle" to be as plentiful as the fish in the sea and acclaiming the excellence of the meat.

Then, having found this great treasure in the new land, the explorers began to slaughter buffaloes indiscriminately and with what seems to be insane enthusiasm. Why? In the main, just for the fun of it. Otherwise sensible

Americans did exactly the same thing more than three hundred years later.

The buffaloes were as easy to shoot as carp in a barrel, even for Spaniards carrying such clumsy primitive weapons as the harquebus and the matchlock musket, many requiring two-man crews. But the inaccuracy and lengthy loading time of these firearms were little handicap in hunting buffalo. The bulls were jammed shoulder-to-shoulder in front of the hunters, who, if they missed the beast they aimed at, were certain to hit another.

Shooting these heavy guns was tiring work, just the same. So one daring conquistador made a thrust at a buffalo with his pike, or spear, and was surprised to see it fall dead. The new technique became a favorite sport, and the slaughter continued with renewed zest. The Spaniards, however, despite their wanton killing, did not appreciably lower the buffalo census, except in California. There were never enough Spaniards in the big buffalo country to inflict a great deal of damage.

In the early days, the buffalo herds ranged in almost every section of the country—from the Atlantic seaboard to the Rockies; from northern Mexico to the subarctic. Like the deer of different regions, they varied in size, color, and other characteristics. Biggest of all was the "woods" buffalo of the Canadian north, the Mackenzie–Great Slave Lake country. A somewhat smaller type roamed the western slopes of the Rockies; there were not many of these, and they disappeared quite early. The East had its coal-black, humpless "Pennsylvania" buffalo, who lived in the hardwood forests and grazed in the adjoining grasslands.

By far the most numerous and important, however, were the magnificent "plains" buffaloes. They ranged over what naturalists believe to have been the original buffalo country —the Midwestern and Western plains from the Mississippi to the Rockies. Although not quite as large as the "woods" type, they were huge animals. A typical full-grown plains bull, about seven years old, stood five and a half or

six feet high at the shoulder and weighed seventeen or eighteen hundred pounds. That was an average weight; some bulls weighed a ton or more.

Most bulls had horns fourteen to fifteen inches long, but many were longer. The record trophy, a Wyoming bull, had horns with an outside length of twenty-two and three eighths inches and a spread of thirty-five and five eighths inches.

The Eastern buffalo was the first to go, since the East was the first area to be fully developed by white settlers. As farmers cleared away the forests the black bison was gradually pushed back. Finally he was driven by hunger to raiding the farms in country in which he had recently foraged. Retaliation was swift and merciless. The settlers classed the bison with the gray wolf as a nuisance and hunted him with the same determination. By 1800 there were only a few left east of the Mississippi; by 1820, none at all. On the other side of the continent the Spanish settlers were busy exterminating the Rocky Mountain type.

One fact became increasingly apparent— the buffalo and civilization could not get along together. The few attempts to domesticate the animal had proved fruitless; and even if it could have been done, there would have been little value in the project. Buffalo meat was definitely inferior to that of the domestic steer, who could graze on the same plains and produce something worth a great deal more. But if the buffalo had been permitted to run wild, he would have continued to be a menace, especially to the farmer. It is easy to imagine what a huge herd of buffalo could do—and frequently did—to a farm, plantation, or ranch. Moreover, the buffalo occupied land that the white man wanted and needed. So the white man took the land away, bit by bit, just as he took it from the Indian.

By 1830, only the plains buffalo remained, but there was a tremendous number of them— fifty million or more. Perhaps one reason he was not seriously threatened earlier was that for many years the endless flat and often tree-

To meet the Eastern demand for buffalo robes, white traders enlisted Indians in the slaughter by offering them whiskey, firearms, and ammunition in exchange for hides.

less plains had been labeled on maps "The Great American Desert." Then some people began to realize that a land which could support fifty million buffaloes and numerous Indians could scarcely be called a desert. It would make good farming land, if no Indians or buffaloes were in the way.

But before the movement to settle the Great Plains began in earnest, a new and unexpected menace to the buffalo arose on the Eastern seaboard of the continent. It was a widespread demand for warm, luxurious buffalo robes, so popular in the days of the horse-drawn carriage and sleigh. To meet this demand white hunters and traders moved out into the Plains in increasing numbers. They not only hunted themselves but enlisted the Indians in the slaughter by offering them cheap whisky, firearms, ammunition, and staples like flour and sugar in exchange for buffalo hides. They often paid little more than a dollar for a skin that could be resold for more than a hundred to the Eastern "carriage trade." There were, of course, numerous middlemen along the way, each of whom took his profit; but for a while there was enough profit for everyone.

Large numbers of Indians began roving the prairies in search of buffaloes beyond their own needs. The braves killed them and the squaws skinned them. Shortly after 1830 the

Frank Mayer used the famous .45/120/550 "Buffalo" Sharps. He estimated that its 120 grains of powder propelled the 550-grain slug at about 1,400 foot seconds, with a muzzle energy of about 2,300 foot pounds.

carnage reached a point where three million buffaloes were being killed in a year. The Civil War finally enforced a lull in this activity, but when the war ended, the final massacre of the buffalo began.

At that time the Plains herds numbered about twenty million, and they ranged from the Kansas and Oklahoma territories west to the Rockies, and from Texas up beyond the Canadian border, moving back and forth each fall and spring for good pasturage. They became the prey of a mass hunt such as had never been seen.

There were many factors that drew so many men to hunt the buffalo. The demand for robes continued. The westward-pushing railroads needed meat for their construction crews. And the end of the war had released a great many young men with new and accurate rifles and good ammunition. Some of these were released soldiers, some ruined Southerners seeking a new start in life; there were also boys from the farms, clerks from the cities, and drifters from everywhere. They carried a weird variety of guns—old cap-and-ball pistols, smoothbore muskets, some Kentucky rifles, big Colt revolvers, percussion-action muzzleloaders such as the "Harpers Ferry" rifle, and the new Hall and Sharps breechloaders.

The word had spread that a man could make his fortune killing buffaloes. "There are millions of them," one Easterner would tell another. "They're easy to kill, and their robes sell for a hundred dollars. What are we waiting for?" The rush began.

Most of these adventurers quickly learned that they could *not* make a fortune killing buffaloes. Most of them could not earn enough to feed themselves. But as fast as one quit, there was another optimist to take his place. At the height of the slaughter, it has been estimated, there were as many as twenty thousand hunters in the field. Among them were a few "sportsmen" who came from the East and from Europe to enjoy the fun. An example of these was an Englishman, Sir George Gore, who arrived in the West in 1854 with an imposing retinue of servants, a private arsenal, and a burning desire to see how many buffaloes he could kill. He hired Jim Bridger, the famous mountain man, as guide and swept into the Wyoming territory for a protracted hunt which produced a bag of twenty-five hundred buffaloes, forty grizzlies, and countless deer, antelope, and elk. The government finally intervened on behalf of the Wyoming Indians, whose food supply was being destroyed before their eyes, but did nothing else to prevent the extermination of the bison. When other important foreign personages indicated a desire to hunt in the West, the government assigned high-ranking Army officers and detachments of cavalry to assist them. One of these was the Grand Duke Alexis of Russia, who in 1871–72 had as his guides and escorts Buffalo Bill Cody, General Custer, and General Sheridan.

Then there were the professional hunters— competent businessmen who had a good-sized investment in equipment. They felt only contempt for the ill-equipped amateurs and the aristocratic sportsmen, and for good reason.

They wanted to keep the buffalo-skin business for themselves rather than see it ruined by men who killed five buffaloes for every skin they managed to take and sell. The professionals shot only as many bulls as their skinners could handle. Why waste effort and ammunition—especially when factory-loaded cartridges sold for twenty-five cents each on the plains? The seasoned skin hunters were frugal; many of them reloaded their own cartridges, some even cast their own bullets.

There were two generally used methods of killing buffaloes—"horse-running" and still-hunting. Since horse-running was spectacular, it was preferred by the so-called sportsman. But it was also used by some skin hunters who had old weapons that lacked long-range power, for they had to get close to their quarry to make a kill.

The procedure was simple. The mounted hunter rode at a gallop directly toward the herd to stampede it. He picked out a good bull, sped along beside it, and shot it in the neck or heart. Then he moved on after the herd and repeated the performance, time after time. A man could kill a large number of buffaloes that way, if his horse did not step into a prairie-dog hole and break his neck. But there was one disadvantage: carcasses were left scattered over a wide area, which made things difficult for the skinners.

Most professional hunters, who accounted for ninety per cent of the skins taken, preferred stillhunting, because this method increased the efficiency of their outfits. The outfit might consist of two or three hunters, six or eight skinners, three or four men to peg out and dry the hides, and a cook. The equipment needed was several wagons, cases of skinning knives and a grindstone to sharpen them, ammunition or the tools to make it, kegs of powder, and the customary camping paraphernalia. These hunters carried the finest rifles they could buy. Sharps were preferred by many of them, Remingtons by others. Nothing but the finest quality powder would do for the reloading of cartridges; some hunters even imported their favorite brands from England.

The hunters might set a daily quota of fifty bulls each, if that was the number the skinners could handle. A good man could usually kill his quota in an hour. The outfit kept on the move, remaining at all times fairly close to a big herd so the hunters could reach it quickly on horseback. When a day's hunt began, the hunters dismounted some distance away and moved in cautiously to avoid stampeding the buffaloes. Then they would take up shooting stations downwind of the herd and about three hundred yards from the nearest animal, keeping quiet and low.

The Remington 40/90 breechloader was another favorite among professional buffalo hunters.

Three hundred yards was the favored range for a number of reasons. First, it decreased the chances of a stampede, for a nearby rifle shot would set the animals running. Second, it gave the hunter a margin of safety in case a stampede broke in his direction. And third, the Remington and Sharps were accurate at that range and were usually sighted for it.

Some hunters shot from a prone position, others sitting—often with crossed sticks as an aid to accuracy. The sticks were slender hickory rods fastened together near the top to form a shallow V. The other ends were sharpened and driven firmly into the earth. With the muzzle placed in the small V, fifty or sixty shots could be fired in short order and with good accuracy.

Frank Mayer, one of the most successful of the skin hunters, always used crossed sticks. He expected—and usually got—a bull for every shot he fired. He was a Sharps enthusiast, although he conceded that the Remington was just as good a rifle. For most of his Plains career, which lasted nine years, he used a .40/90 Sharps, but later switched to the fa-

To clear the track of buffaloes, trainmen and passengers would shoot the animals from the train, leaving hundreds to rot on the plains.

mous "Buffalo" Sharps, the .45/120/550. He paid two hundred dollars for his rifle—a big price in a time when a workingman earned ten or twelve dollars a week. That weapon, in his hands, meant sudden death even far beyond the range Mayer usually chose, three hundred yards. He estimated that its 120 grains of powder propelled the 550-grain slug at about 1,400 foot seconds, with a muzzle energy of about 2,300 foot pounds. That was a tremendous striking power.

When he was positioned at three hundred yards from a herd, Mayer started his day's work by shooting a cow through the lungs. She would stumble and stagger and cough up blood. Then the bulls, excited by the blood scent, would move in and hook her viciously with their horns. While they were occupied, the hunter could pick them off one by one. Frequently Mayer shot down his entire daily quota of fifty from one spot. But if the herd stampeded, he followed it patiently and started all over again.

When his fiftieth buffalo was down, Mayer summoned the wagon train, and the skinners took over. With such a hunter, they usually found all their carcasses lying inside an area three hundred feet square. While they worked, the hunter cleaned his rifle, reloaded ammunition, and loafed. Collecting two or three dollars each for his skins, Mayer probably earned as much as any other hunter. But at the end of nine years, he found that he had netted only three thousand dollars a year. It cost a great deal to maintain a wagon outfit and to pay skinners and other helpers. Some hunters maintained that they never netted more than twenty dollars a week. If anyone got rich in the buffalo trade, it was the men who ran the big fur-trading houses.

They handled a prodigious number of skins. One firm in St. Louis, Missouri, shipped two hundred and fifty thousand hides to the East in a single year. In Fort Worth, Texas, two hundred thousand were sold in a one-day auction. A Dodge City, Kansas, company shipped two hundred thousand the first year the railroad reached town; other local firms freighted hundreds of tons of hides that same year, plus two hundred carloads of hind-quarters and many carloads of tongues. With the extension of the railroads and the establishment of new Army posts in the West, the market for buffalo meat increased even more. One contract hunter, Buffalo Bill Cody, is said to have killed 4,280 bulls in 1868 and 1869. But most of the meat was wasted because the laborers would eat only the best cuts.

When the Union Pacific reached Cheyenne in 1867, its east–west line cut the Great Plains in two and divided the plains buffaloes into two mammoth herds, northern and southern. The southern buffaloes were doomed first, because the Santa Fe Railroad reached the heart of the summer range in 1871, providing much better shipping facilities. Still, Colonel R. I. Dodge, a reputable observer, reported seeing one herd of about four million buffaloes at about this time. The hunters worked hard; between 1871 and 1875 they killed two and a half million buffaloes in the Kansas territory alone. By 1875, the entire southern herd had been just about exterminated. And by this time, too, the price of buffalo robes had dropped drastically. The market had been oversupplied, and lined buffalo robes were advertised in Eastern cities for a little as nine dollars. Hunters were lucky to get sixty-five to seventy-five cents for a skin.

But still the slaughter continued, some of it carried out by train crews and passengers. Sometimes great herds would saunter across the tracks, completely blocking a train's path. A few foolhardy engineers tried to charge the beasts with their locomotives, which were derailed without much damage to the buffaloes. Train crews began to carry rifles, and so did the passengers. If a train came upon a herd, the engineer would obligingly stop, whether beasts blocked his way or not. Then all hands would get out of the cars and start shooting at

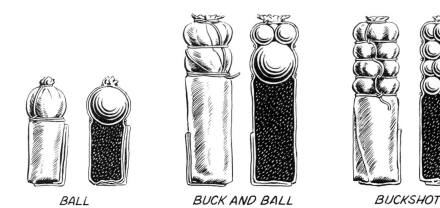

BALL   BUCK AND BALL   BUCKSHOT

The first cartridges were simple paper rolls enclosing one or more round bullets and a charge of powder. The hunter would tear or bite open the cartridge, pour the powder down the barrel, then ram the bullet down with the paper wadded on top.

the buffaloes. Hundreds of animals were killed and left to rot, while hundreds more were seriously wounded and would die later. If the passengers had any ammunition left, they shot from the windows as the train got under way again.

After the southern herd had been wiped out, the professional hunters moved north and began the final massacre of the bison. On New Year's Day, 1872, there were about seven million animals in the northern herd. By the end of the year, four million had been killed. In 1873, another million died. Each hunter was trying to outdo the next one in getting the last few animals. By 1877, only five hundred thousand buffaloes remained in the northern herd, and by 1885 only seventy-five thousand.

In 1889, with less than two hundred buffaloes left, the government decided to "protect" them. Today the herds have increased to safer levels and once more are hunted in certain areas. But only as a "one-to-a-customer" game animal.

The decline of the buffalo, from 1840 to 1889, was paralleled by great progress in rifle design, and above all in ammunition for rifles.

Hall's breech-loading rifle had been improved by Sharps, Remington, and other

manufacturers, which opened the door for the elongated bullet. That bullet, in turn, speeded the development of the modern cartridge. And the cartridge led to the creation of the repeating rifle.

Gunsmiths and hunters had known for some time that a small round ball was more accurate than a large one, but it lacked striking power. And they had searched for a way to combine the two features, the result being the elongated bullet, of small diameter but plenty of weight. Some men had made conical bullets that could be forced down the barrel of a muzzle-loader, but they came upon this idea just about the time the breechloader replaced the older guns. A rifle like the Sharps, however, could easily take a conical bullet loaded from the breech. Sharps himself put out such a bullet in a paper cartridge—a tube containing black powder in one end and the bullet in the other. When the action was closed, after loading, the ascending breechblock sheared the paper tail off the cartridge so that the powder would be exposed for the percussion flash. Later, Sharps marketed a linen cartridge, which was more dependable.

Meanwhile, other inventors were experimenting with metallic cartridges. One was Dr. Edward Maynard, the dentist who had in-

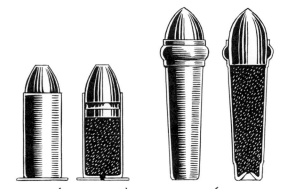

SHARPS (PAPER)   SHARPS (LINEN)   MAYNARD (METALLIC)   BURNSIDE (METALLIC)

Early Sharps cartridges were paper with conical bullets, but later a stronger cartridge made of linen was developed and became popular along with the Sharps breechloader. The cartridge covers were made inflammable and the entire case could be loaded unopened and the fire of the newly developed percussion cap ignited it.

The Burnside cartridge had a brass case with a small hole in the base to admit fire from the percussion cap in a breech-loading gun. The Maynard, another cartridge used with a percussion cap, was one of the first brass cartridges that could be reloaded and used many times. The large base was used to extract the shell after firing.

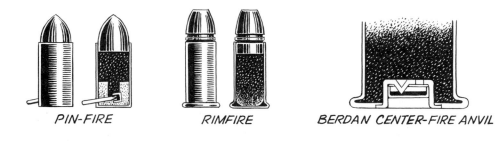

PIN-FIRE   RIMFIRE   BERDAN CENTER-FIRE ANVIL

Self-exploding cartridges contained the ignition in the cartridge itself. One common type was the pin-fire, with a percussion cap inside the head of the cartridge. The cap had a protruding pin which rested in the detonating compound and fired the powder when struck by the gun's hammer. The rimfire cartridge held the detonating powder in the rim of the cartridge head, and when the rim was pinched by the firing pin, it exploded the powder. The center-fire cartridge had a tiny cup filled with priming mixture in the center of the cartridge base. Near it in Berdan's cartridge was a piece of metal called the "anvil." When the rifleman pulled the trigger, the firing pin drove the primer against the anvil and exploded the powder.

vented the tapelock percussion system. In 1851 he introduced a cartridge consisting of a small brass tube soldered to a flat base. Powder was poured into the open end and a bullet inserted tightly. A pinhole in the side of the case conducted the percussion flash to the black powder. Another cartridge, the Burnside, which won praise in the Civil War, was similar to the Maynard but had it percussion hole in the base.

The first complete cartridge—one containing bullet, powder, and priming—was introduced by Smith & Wesson in 1859. It was a rimfire, not unlike the one used in today's .22-caliber rifles. Smith & Wesson made the old percussion cap the base of its new cartridge; when the firing pin pinched the rim of the base it set off the primer—fulminate of mercury—which at once fired the powder.

The first Smith & Wesson cartridge had one major defect, its case was made of soft copper and was not safe with heavy charges of powder. But in 1869 Colonel Henry Berdan devised a practical method of "drawing" brass—forming strong, seamless cases from solid metal. Brass proved to be almost the ideal material for cartridges. It was slightly elastic, expanding just enough under an explosion to help seal in the powder gases, which had always been a problem with breechloaders.

Colonel Berdan soon joined forces with an inventive genius, Marcellus Hartley of the Union Metallic Cartridge Company. Together, they developed the center-fire cartridge. Now their method seems simple, but its development required long and patient experimentation. In the center of a cartridge base they placed a tiny cup filled with the priming mixture. Near it they set a piece of metal called the "anvil." When the rifleman pulled the trigger, the firing pin drove the cup of primer against the anvil and exploded it. The flash then ignited the powder.

The modern cartridge had been born. But two other revolutionary improvements were to follow in the next few years—the repeating rifle and smokeless powder.

CHAPTER 10

The Golden Age of Big-Game Hunting

The thirty years between 1870 and 1900 can well be called the Golden Age of American big-game hunting for many reasons. There was a still-abundant supply of game that provided superlative sport; there were many important improvements in firearms; and railroads opened up the big-game country of the West so that hunting for fun became a democratic sport that many could enjoy, not just an amusement restricted to a few wealthy men.

Even east of the Mississippi there was still much game. Although years of ruthless meat hunting had reduced the deer population greatly, the flash of a whitetail's flag was still an often-recurring thrill to the hunter who worked the hardwood thickets of New England and the Middle Atlantic states, the laurel tangles of the Southern mountains, or the vast woods of the Great Lakes region. And where there were deer, there were usually black bears. Moose were plentiful in most of Eastern Canada and in the Maine woods, and each October meat hunters and sportsmen alike took a heavy toll from the thousands of caribou that migrated southward across Newfoundland.

It was the West of the 1870s and 1880s, however, that was the hunter's paradise. Although the buffalo were fast being exterminated, the meat hunters had as yet scarcely touched the other species of Western game. Deer were plentiful—water-loving whitetails under the shadow of the cottonwoods in the river bottoms; mule deer (which the men who hunted them usually called blacktails) in quiet pockets in the foothills, among the stunted pines and twisted cedars on rugged mountainsides, and on the high deserts. In most districts grizzly bears were growing scarce, but there were still enough of them to satisfy a hunter who searched for such tough adversaries. There were huge herds of elk high up in the Rockies, and smaller herds in the foothills and sometimes right out on the open plains.

Bighorn sheep and nimble-hoofed mountain goats dared the sportsman to match his nerve and stamina against theirs on dizzying crags. And on color-splashed Southern mesas and high Northern prairies there were great bands of wary, keen-eyed antelope who could run faster than any but a top quarter horse and who asked only that they see the hunter before he saw them. Outside of Africa, the West of those years was the greatest big-game country in the world.

After the Civil War this abundant game began to attract an increasing number of sportsmen. While waterfowl and upland-bird shooting had been sports in the East and South since colonial days, most men—until about 1870—who went out with their rifles were looking for meat, not sport. In the West until that time, almost the only sport hunters were a few Army officers trying to relieve the boredom of Indian-country garrison duty, and an occasional wealthy foreigner who could afford a wagon train manned by a retinue of professional hunters, guides, teamsters, and horse wranglers. Only a few of the pioneers and settlers whose courage and hard work pushed the frontier farther and farther westward had time or desire to hunt for sport. To them the rifle was as much a tool as ax or plow—a triple-use tool with which they protected themselves against Indians, tried to clear predators out of newly opened sections, and got meat for their cook pots.

The coming of the railroads to the West opened the era of sport hunting for everybody. The first transcontinental line was completed in 1869 when the Union Pacific joined the Central Pacific near Ogden, Utah. During the next fifteen years more than a hundred thousand miles of steel were laid, much of it west of the Mississippi. Using the railroads, a man who was neither frontiersman nor millionaire could hunt the abundant game of the post Civil War West.

Meanwhile, the arms manufacturers worked hard to provide the increasing number of sportsmen with better rifles for hunting. The rifle used by the Western big-game hunter of the early seventies was usually a single-shot weapon. There were a few Spencer and Henry Civil War repeaters, but they were rare. If the hunter was a wealthy British sportsman, his weapon was usually a double-barreled rifle designed for East Indian or

As the demand for more and better rifles increased, a man could drop into a country store and find just the model he was looking for.

African game, for which he had paid between the equivalent of seven hundred-fifty and a thousand dollars and which probably bore one of the world-famous names, Purdey, Greener, or Holland. If the hunter was a settler out for meat or a tenderfoot looking for a thrill, he might carry any of several popular single-shots—perhaps a Maynard or a Peabody.

But if he was a professional or an experienced big-game hunter, he shot either a Remington or a Sharps—and the odds were heavily in favor of its being a Sharps for which he had paid between thirty and seventy dollars. Frank H. Mayer, the famous buffalo hunter, had half a dozen Sharps; the one he bought last and liked best was a custom-made .45/120/550 that had "Special Old Reliable" stamped on its barrel and which cost him two hundred and thirty-seven dollars. Colonel W. D. Pickett, a Confederate veteran who moved to Wyoming and hunted big bears for sport, shot a .45/110/340 Sharps with such devastating effect that of the twenty-three grizzlies he killed in a single season, only six of the hulking animals required more than one bullet.

But even those Sharps enthusiasts who were good enough to make a kill with almost every shot were not entirely satisfied with the single-shot rifle. The arms manufacturers and inventors, realizing that a good repeater would have a tremendous sale, were experimenting to give the hunters what they wanted before a competitor did.

The repeating rifle idea was not new. For more than a quarter of a century firearms designers had been trying to develop a successful one. Among the earliest was Colonel Samuel Colt, who in the late 1830s had adapted his revolver cylinder to a rifle action and then produced several improvements on his original model. But his revolving-cylinder rifle did not meet wide approval, nor did similar weapons produced by other makers. In 1860, however, two practical, repeating

lever-action rifles were patented—just in time to play a part in the Civil War.

One was the Spencer, a rifle or carbine using a .56-caliber rimfire cartridge. Its seven-cartridge, straight-line magazine was built into the stock, and it was capable of fifteen shots a minute. Nearly a hundred thousand Spencers were manufactured for the Union forces, and the soldiers—mostly cavalrymen—to whom they were issued considered themselves very fortunate.

The other early repeater was the Henry, a .44-caliber rifle which had a fifteen-cartridge, tube magazine under its barrel, the cartridges being carried to the chamber by a conveyer block operated by a lever. About ten thousand Henrys were manufactured for the Northern forces, and the few men who got them liked them. The Confederate soldiers had quite a different view, calling the new repeater "that damned Yankee rifle that is loaded on Sunday and fired all week."

In 1866 Oliver F. Winchester, a Connecticut textile manufacturer who had been in financial control of the firm making the Henrys for the government, decided to start manufacturing firearms under his own name. He bought the Spencer patents, not because he wanted to use them but to eliminate competition. He also controlled the patents on the Henry rifle, and hired B. Tyler Henry, its inventor, to improve it. The Henry action proved so dependable and popular that it was used in all of the long line of successful lever-action repeaters which for a quarter of a century made the name "Winchester" almost synonymous with the word "rifle." The *H* that is still stamped on all Winchester rimfire ammunition is the company's tribute to its pioneering designer.

The first Winchester, the Model 1866, was an improved version of the Civil War Henry military rifle. In seven years, a hundred and seventy thousand were sold, but a large share of them were military weapons bought by the Turkish government. The .44 rimfire cartridge

The Winchester 1873 was designed to fire the heavier center-fire cartridges. This 44-caliber, twelve-shot repeater was popular with the deer hunters of the East, but was considered by many to be too light for the big game of the West.

for which the 1866 was chambered probably lacked sufficient power to satisfy most Western hunters.

So at the beginning of the Golden Age of hunting in 1870, the repeating rifle was available, but the men who killed most of the big game were still doing it with the old single-shot Sharps and Remingtons. Yet ten years later these same time-tested guns were being offered for sale at about a quarter of their original prices, with so few buyers that eventually many of them fell into the hands of the Indians.

The reason for the lack of interest in the single-shot actions was the development of the sensationally successful second Winchester model, introduced in 1873. It was a .44-caliber, twelve-shot repeater which looked and was very much like the Model 1866. The principal changes were strengthening of the mechanism and the adaptation of the parts to handle the heavier center fire cartridges.

The Model 1873 attracted a great deal of attention and aroused plenty of controversy. Everyone who shot a rifle talked about it. Some hunters hailed it as a near-perfect weapon. Others condemned it as a mere popgun. There were no neutrals. In general, Eastern sportsmen welcomed it. Most of them had been hunting their deer with single-shot weapons that even included muzzle-loading Springfield muskets, and consequently had seen many wounded whitetails whisk into the thickets to be lost. A repeater would enable them to get in a second or even a third shot when necessary, and the .44 W.C.F. cartridge carried enough power to kill them.

Most Western hunters, however, brought up in the heavy-load, big-bullet tradition, were skeptical about the new gun. They admitted that it would be fine against Eastern deer, but would it stop a buffalo or a grizzly?

From the ballistics point of view, they had sound reason for doubt. The .44 W.C.F. cartridge, with its 200-grain bullet propelled by 40 grains of black powder, had a muzzle velocity of 1,245 foot seconds, as compared to the Sharps .45 caliber rifle, with a 550-grain bullet propelled by 120 grains of powder and a muzzle velocity of 1,400 foot seconds. The Sharps therefore delivered almost three times as much lead a little faster. That ended the argument temporarily, so far as most Western big-game hunters were concerned, but a few of the more open-minded men experimented with the Winchester "popgun"—sometimes with surprising results.

One of these was Frank Mayer, the buffalo hunter. One Sunday morning he took a busman's holiday to try out the gun on jack rabbits. He ran into a group of seven buffaloes. Riding up close and holding the Winchester handgun-fashion, he dropped one bull with his first shot. Then in the course of a mile run he killed the six others, and only three required a second bullet.

Three years later Winchester ended the argument by giving the big-gun hunters just what they wanted—the Model 1876, a twelve-shot, enlarged version of the Model 1873, chambered for the Winchester .45/75 cartridge with a 350-grain bullet. Then in 1879 and in 1885, Winchester brought out six-shot .45/70 military and sporting Hotchkiss models. They were the first bolt-action repeaters made in America. Many hunters liked the sporting model, but not enough of them for the gun ever to threaten the supremacy of the lever-action rifle.

As soon as the popularity of the repeater was assured, Winchester began to manufacture large numbers of rifles each year, using the interchangeable-parts and mass-production methods devised by Eli Whitney, Samuel

Colt, and Christian Sharps. And as rifle production went up, rifle prices came down. No longer did a hunter have to pay forty or fifty dollars for a dependable weapon. Now he could buy one for fifteen to twenty dollars, a price within the budgets of hundreds of thousands of potential hunters.

Two new transcontinental railroads, the Northern Pacific and the Great Northern, were pushed across the Plains and over the Rockies, making it possible for many of these new hunters with good repeaters to travel to the wonderful big-game country. The Northern Pacific ran through the heart of the Flathead–Kootenai region of Montana, which until that time could be reached only by a long and expensive wagon or pack-horse out-

fit. Outfitters in the railroad towns rented horses and camping equipment and provided guides. Sportsmen traveled a circular route which brought them back to the railroad after two or three weeks in grizzly-bear, elk, and moose country.

For years the hunting was so good that even a tenderfoot soon found that getting a whitetail or a mule deer was a mere camp chore. But when a man started out after deer, he never knew what he might run into before he got back to camp. If it happened to be a grizzly, he was very happy to have a repeater with plenty of power. But there were many other kinds of big game he might encounter. Although the great herds of buffalo were almost gone, there were still many small bands

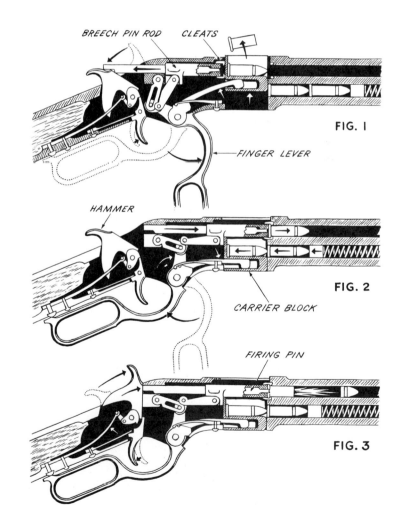

The Winchester 1873 mechanism operated as follows: The finger lever was pressed forward (Fig. 1), pulling back the breech pin rod, causing small cleats at the tip of the rod to pull the empty casing back with the rod, extracting it from the chamber. At the same time the lever action forced the hammer back, cocked the trigger, and forced the carrier block upward, raising a new shell to the level of the chamber. Returning the finger level to its original position (Fig. 2) forced the breech pin rod forward, pushing the cartridge into the barrel, and at the same time lowered the carrier block to receive another cartridge. The trigger and hammer were in cocked position at this stage. Pulling the trigger (Fig. 3) released the hammer against the breech pin rod, causing the firing pin to detonate the cartridge.

left. An old bull's "scalp," as the head was called, made a fine trophy. Elk, once so plentiful on the plains that they had been "run" like buffalo by mounted hunters, were still easy to find in the mountains; and since they were subject to fits of panic, meat hunters could sometimes slaughter twenty or more of a band of a hundred.

Hunting grizzlies, buffaloes, elk, or antelope was full of thrills, but the bighorn mountain sheep was the West's most prized trophy. The bighorn offered a real challenge. It lived in high and rugged places, where hunting it required steel muscles and plenty of wind. Its eyes were as sharp as an antelope's, and its nose and ears as keen as an elk's. It could climb a steep, rock-cluttered slope in a flash, and bound down a sheer cliff like a rubber ball. Sometimes the hunter won the contest, but more often he lost.

A ram gave one sportsman who had killed every other Western big-game species the biggest surprise and the most embarrassing moment of his long hunting career. High in the mountains he spotted the sheep through his field glasses and, after a long, difficult stalk got within a hundred yards of it. Just as he was about to shoot, he felt a breeze on the back of his neck and knew that the wind had shifted. Before he could get his double-barreled rifle up the ram winded him and vanished.

Later in the day he came upon the tracks of the same ram in the snow and followed them. As he edged around a juniper he saw the bighorn climbing a steep, rocky slope. By the time the hunter had raised his rifle, the ram was standing on the skyline a hundred and twenty-five yards away. It was not a difficult shot, but the man missed—with both barrels. The ram ducked over the ridge.

Glancing up as he finished reloading, the disgusted sportsman saw the bighorn backtracking, at a gallop, right toward him. He waited until it was only fifteen feet away, then he jumped up. The astonished ram reared. Coolly the hunter stuck the rifle almost in its face and pressed one trigger, then the other. Nothing happened! He had forgotten to cock either hammer. The ram dodged past him and disappeared.

Game was so plentiful in the eighteen eighties that men who started out for deer might come up against a couple of grizzlies instead.

Winchester had everything its own way in the repeating-rifle field through the 1870s, but early in the eighties other manufacturers, spurred by the big demand for sporting firearms, began to offer serious competition. The first challenge to Winchester supremacy was the Remington-Keene eight-shot repeater, which had a tube-type magazine and a bolt action and was chambered for .45/70 and .44/40 cartridges. It was a high-class rifle, but it failed to win wide popularity, perhaps because it was difficult to clean; its manufacture was discontinued after a few years. Marlin produced a .45/70 lever-action repeater in 1881 and from 1888 on introduced a new model almost every year through the nineties. They were good rifles and became very popular.

Winchester answered the competition with its Model 1886—as smooth-working a lever-action rifle as has ever been built. It was a nine-shot weapon which at first was chambered for the .45/70 cartridge and subsequently for others, including the .50/110/300, the heaviest and highest-powered load that was available at that time.

The next Winchester big-game rifle was the Model 1892, a fifteen-shot lever action handling .25-, .32-, .38-, and .44-caliber loads. Before this excellent deer rifle was discontinued in 1937, more than a million had been sold, and many of them are still getting game for their owners.

By the middle 1880s, many hunters found that they had to go farther and work harder to get big game. Wheat and corn were being grown on many thousands of acres of what a decade earlier had been virgin prairie. The buffalo was almost gone, the elk had been driven into the high hills, and even deer and antelope were thinning out because of the merciless killing of market hunters who sold the meat and skins in towns along the railroads. Cattle outfits fed their cowhands venison, and saw nothing wrong about it. "We raise steers to sell," they said, "and kill deer to eat."

The great increase in sport hunting was an added menace to the game. Some of the men who prided themselves on being sportsmen took an enthusiastic part in shooting a

hundred or more sleeping wild turkeys out of their roosting trees, and similar cold-blooded exploits. The states that had game laws made little, if any, effort to enforce them.

Theodore Roosevelt, ranching where the Little Missouri runs through the badlands near the North Dakota–Montana line, told how he killed what he knew to be the last elk left in that part of the country—told it without apology or shame. Later he was to spearhead the conservation movement, sponsoring the sound doctrine that game is a renewable natural resource which we can always have if only we have enough common sense not to kill it faster than it can be replenished. But this was a startling concept to most people, and a difficult one to make convincing. In 1885 the idea prevailed that as the West was settled the game would have to go. If the game was to be wiped out by civilization, most settlers, meat hunters, and sportsmen felt they might as well get their share while they could. So the game was being destroyed—fast.

East of the Mississippi conditions were even worse because there men had been hunting game for a much longer time. Market hunters were killing thousands of deer each year. Every fall large numbers of sport hunters invaded New York's Adirondacks and other deer regions; in the late eighties there were enough sport camps in the Maine woods to make publishing a directory of them a profitable venture. Reputable hunters engaged in practices that would put them in jail today. Chasing deer into the lakes and then shooting or clubbing them to death from canoes was standard procedure in the Adirondacks. Hunting deer at night with lights, at first with a birchbark torch and later with a reflector lantern, was legitimate. The stealthy paddle along the shadowy river bank or lake shore, the gleam of the quarry's eyes in the dark, the quick shot before the light-fascinated deer could bound away—such hunting had an allure which made many hunters hate to give

it up. But, to their credit, many did so—realizing that it was unsportsmanlike—long before it was declared illegal.

In the middle nineties, after many of the Eastern deer were killed off and all species of Western big game became dangerously depleted, sportsmen all over the country began to realize what was happening. They demanded that something drastic be done at once to save what was left of the game and to help it increase, and that game laws should be made stricter and be more strictly enforced.

Still, improvements in guns and ammunition continued. The next big step forward was the development of smokeless powder. Black powder had long been essentially the same mixture of charcoal, sulphur, and saltpeter whose explosive properties had been demonstrated by Roger Bacon in the Middle Ages. In military rifles, black powder had the obvious disadvantage of giving away a soldier's position to the enemy. In any rifle, it soon fouled the barrel and burned so close to instantaneously that the gas pressure, which propels the bullet, began to decrease even before the bullet left the barrel. This progressively decreasing pressure kept muzzle velocities below 2,000 foot seconds, with resulting high trajectories and loss of power by the time the bullet reached its mark. Moreover, a hunter often had difficulty getting off second or third shots because of the cloud of dark smoke that obscured his vision.

For more than half a century men had tried to make a more efficient propellant. In 1846, guncotton was made by treating cotton with a mixture of nitric and sulphuric acids. In the late seventies a smokeless powder was produced by compounding guncotton with inorganic nitrates; it was an instant success as a shotgun powder, but it burned too fast for use in rifles. In the eighties Alfred Nobel made ballistite by gelatinizing guncotton with nitroglycerin; and two Britishers developed cordite, a smokeless powder still used in

Most old timers had little use for scope
sights, which became popular after 1900.

England, composed of gelatinized guncotton,
nitroglycerin, and mineral jelly. At about the
same time a French chemist, L. J. G. Vieille,
produced a slow-burning smokeless powder
by incorporating guncotton with a mixture of
ether and alcohol and rolling the resulting
paste into thin sheets which were cut into
small squares. An improvement of his process,
in which the paste is mechanically extruded
into perforated cylindrical grains, was used
in making American smokeless powder.

The first sporting rifle designed to fire the
new smokeless-powder ammunition was the
Winchester Model 1894. It had an eight-shot,
tube magazine, a new lever action, a new
nickel-steel barrel, and it used the brand new

.30/30 cartridge—the notable "thirty-thirty"
that became famous everywhere in America
that game was hunted. The comparatively
slow-burning smokeless powder used in this
cartridge kept the gas pressure increasing
until just before the bullet left the barrel, and
gave it a muzzle velocity of more than 2,000
feet a second. The Model 1894 also was chambered for .38- and .32-caliber black-powder
cartridges, and in 1895 for the .32 Winchester
Special and the .25/35 Winchester, both
smokeless loads. Well over a million of these
rifles were sold in the next thirty years and are
still popular as carbine models.

For some years a few big-game hunters
had experimented with telescopic sights.

Frank Mayer used imported 20X sights on two of his Sharps buffalo guns. But they had not become widely popular. Now, with rifles of comparatively high velocity and low trajectory, there was new interest in scopes, but they were not easily available to the average rifle owner until, shortly after 1900, the Stevens company absorbed a firm which specialized in popular-priced scope sights.

In 1895 Winchester introduced a sporting version of the Lee Straight Pull, a military bolt-action rifle, manufactured for the Navy, which had a box magazine and was the first clip-loader. Savage brought out a lever-action rifle, chambered for the new smokeless ammunition, which led to the Model 99 with its hammerless solid breech and rotary magazine.

So, at the end of the Golden Age of American hunting, the modern high-velocity hunting rifle was born, and the first demand for the protection of our diminishing game had come from sportsmen all over the country.

CHAPTER 11

"Shooting Flying"

Although the land the early American colonists came to was rich in game, the hard work of making a living and subduing a wilderness left them little time for any kind of sport. They shot upland birds and waterfowl, but they shot them in the way that was most certain to provide food and save expensive powder and shot. They crept up on them and shot them sitting.

Until about midway in the seventeen seventies, that was the way most British and European bird hunters did their shooting too, although most of them were wealthy landowners and did not have to worry about getting a meal with their guns. Some hunters tried to emulate the unknown Italian who, in 1580, brought down a flying bird, but few succeeded. The time lag between the pressing of the trigger of a wheellock or snaphance smoothbore and its discharge was so long and unpredictable that an accurate estimate of the distance to lead a flying bird was almost impossible. Only a rare shot would, by luck, hit its mark. Shooting flying continued to be largely a waste of gunpowder until the more dependable flintlock appeared in the middle sixteen hundreds. After that, wing-shooting gained in popularity slowly but steadily in England, and a hundred years later few Britishers who called themselves sportsmen would shoot at a grouse or pheasant except when it was in the air.

Probably the oldest bird-shooting gun in existence is a snaphance smoothbore, labeled a "birding piece" and dated 1614, which once belonged to King Charles I and is now in the Tower of London arms collection. From the appearance and weight of this antique scattergun it is obvious that its royal owner must have used it to amuse himself by picking off sitting birds. For more than a century after it was made, fowling pieces continued to be heavy, long-barreled single guns with a musketlike fore-end that extended to within an inch or two of the muzzle.

Credit for much of the early development that paved the way for the modern shotgun must go to an English genius named Joseph Manton who improved the smoothbore into a weapon which, in appearance at least, compares favorably with the best of today's guns. Manton was one of the first gunsmiths—possibly the first—to make double-barreled game guns. The barrels of the early double-guns were joined merely by narrow metal bridges spaced along them. Manton soon introduced the now-familiar top rib and did an effective streamlining job that gave his guns an almost modern look.

By the early eighteen hundreds, English shotgun making had grown into a thriving business. In 1812 there were forty-seven makers of sporting arms in London alone. Prices ran as high as the equivalent of $350, an amount of considerably greater value than it is now. Cheap guns were not made because there was no market for them. The British idea that game belongs to the owner of the land that produces it, backed up by severe penalties for poaching, restricted shooting to rich landowners and their guests.

For a quarter of a century or more, Manton was the most successful of the many gunsmiths trying to improve the shotgun. When, in 1807, Alexander Forsyth patented the use of fulminating salts to fire gunpowder, Manton was quick to appreciate its possibilities. After several years of experimenting he brought out a lock in which an ax-shaped hammerhead struck a small copper tube, which was filled with detonating powder, and was located in the barrel's touchhole.

The lock was effective but was soon supplanted by a more convenient device in which a thimble-shaped, copper cup, or cap, holding a small quantity or fulminate of mercury, was placed over a hollow nipple connected to the powder chamber. This percussion cap was revolutionary, but it wasn't patented. Its invention is usually credited to the American artist, Joshua Shaw, but some historians believe that Manton first developed it. In any event, Forsyth sued Manton for the use of his percussion lock and won his case. This brought about Manton's financial ruin, and he died bankrupt in 1835. But he had trained apprentices who founded four London gunmaking establishments which are still manufacturing first-class shotguns.

One of the concepts that the American colonists left behind in England was that wild game belongs to the landowner. They believed that while game is alive it belongs to nobody and everybody, and that after it is dead it belongs to the man who killed it. Such a belief was essential in the wilderness of the New World because most settlers were dependent upon game for much of their food. And in time, the idea would make sport hunting a popular democratic amusement.

When today's scattergunner looks back on those early days, it makes him feel that he was born a couple of centuries too late. Except in an occasional lean year, the woods were heavily populated with wild turkeys. In spring and fall the seacoast bays and inland rivers were carpeted with millions of migrating waterfowl. Ruffed grouse, the "partridge" of the Northern colonies, were almost as plentiful as bobwhite quail, the "partridge" of the South. Each October great flights of woodcock started their long journeys from Canada to the Gulf Coast. Most numerous of all were the passenger pigeons, whose seemingly endless flights darkened the sun for minutes at a time as they passed.

Most of the colonists enjoyed hunting, but their chief motive was meat. When they could, the settlers trapped or netted upland birds, or killed them with stones and clubs. When they had to shoot to get them, they used an old flintlock musket that would throw a load of shot or even rusty nails. Some of the Pennsylvania German gunsmiths made brass-barreled smoothbores for bird shooting, but there was little demand for such specialized guns.

As the forests were cleared, farming increased and villages grew into towns and cities. Hunting conditions changed as a result. Game continued to be plentiful, but not quite so plentiful as it had been. By 1770 twelve of the thirteen colonies found it necessary to establish closed seasons, although they were almost as short as open seasons today. A man had to travel farther to get a whitetail or a bag of birds, and many townsmen bought their game from market hunters. Big land-owners began to save the game on their estates by enforcing trespass laws and being strict with poachers.

In 1790 a son-in-law of Benjamin Franklin released some Hungarian partridges on his country place in New Jersey—the first new game species introduced into America. Wealthy Americans visiting England were attracted to the idea of shooting birds on the wing for *sport*—and brought back high-priced English double-barreled guns for that purpose. By the beginning of the eighteen hundreds shooting flying birds had become a recognized sport which, if slowly, was winning popularity.

Henry William Herbert, who under the pen name of Frank Forester was America's first widely read sports writer, told of an October day in the early eighteen thirties when he and two companions went shooting some fifty miles from New York City. Their bag for the day was fifty-three woodcock, twenty-four quail, and five ruffed grouse. And they were shooting muzzle-loaders!

By 1850 the muzzle-loading shotgun had become an efficient game killer, but was a difficult and even dangerous weapon to fire. The sportsman had to carry powder flasks, shot pouches, wads, and percussion caps. He had to measure the correct powder charges into each gun barrel, ram wads down on them, pour in just the right amount of shot, ram wads over it, raise the hammers to half-cock, and replace the used percussion caps with new ones before he could fire.

This complicated loading procedure caused exasperating delays when birds were flying, and many tragic accidents occurred when hunters tried to hurry. Now and then one gun barrel would go off while the other was being loaded and the unlucky hunter might lose a hand. Overeager hunters forgot

Shooting a Chinese ringneck pheasant was a rare event for several years after 1887, when it was first imported and released; now it is a common game bird.

to remove the ramrod, or loaded both charges of powder into the same barrel—usually with unfortunate results.

In 1850 Lefaucheux, a French gunmaker, introduced a pin-fire cartridge and a double gun that was the direct ancestor of those we use today. His cartridge case contained powder, shot, and a percussion cap. A thin pin, one of its ends centered in the cap and the other protruding through the cartridge case and the gun barrel, detonated the fulminate of mercury in the cap when the hammer struck it. The gun developed by Lefaucheux had no extractor. The hunter opened it by means of a lever under its fore-end operating a crude prototype of the now-universal hinge action, yanked the fired cases out with a small hooked tool, and loaded new cartridges into the breech.

The following year Joseph Lang, a leading London gunmaker, introduced the Lefaucheux gun in England and created a great controversy. Progressive-minded sportsmen welcomed it. Conservatives scoffed at it as "that French crutch gun" (because of its hinge) and predicted that after a few days in

the field it would shoot so loose that it would be suicide to fire it. A few acknowledged the great advantages of breech-loading but criticized the gas leakage that kept the new gun from shooting as hard as a tightly wadded muzzle-loader. Lang soon overcome that objection by modifying the Lefaucheux action to one in which a bolt forced the barrels back upon projections on the standing breech which fitted into the chambers, forming a gas-tight breech. Another prominent craftsman brought out a gun which used a center-fire cartridge (which quickly supplanted the pin-fire).

Captain Adam H. Bogardus patented a trap for hurling glass balls into the air. In 1877 he broke 1,000 balls in 101 minutes; another time he broke 5,000 in 500 minutes.

Doubts about the breechloader's game-killing effectiveness persisted, however, and in 1859 the controversy was intensified by public trials in which muzzle-loaders gave a little more penetration than did breechloaders using heavy powder charges. In the eighteen sixties this single drawback was overcome through the introduction of the choke—that slight constriction of the muzzle end of a shotgun bore which concentrates the charge of lead pellets and increases their velocity and striking power. The choke bore seems to have been developed independently in England by Pape and in America by Fred Kimble, a well-known market hunter.

Other improvements and refinements—including an ejector which flipped the used shells clear of the chambers when it was opened for reloading— followed quickly, until in the early eighteen seventies the double-gun, in its mechanical essentials, was the same weapon that we shoot today.

Toward the end of that decade, when the breech-loading shotgun was becoming more widely known in America, a good deal of the wildness had been removed from many parts of the American Wild West. Threatened less by Indians and outlaws, frontier people had a little more opportunity to enjoy themselves, and even some of the old-timers who had always sneered at the shotgun as a "dude's grasshopper killer" found that shooting grouse with one could be a lot of fun. Eastern sportsmen, too, who had gone West to hunt big game, sent home for their scatterguns and had some of the finest bird shooting of their lives.

Western grouse hunters had their choice of two varieties—the sharptail grouse that were retreating as civilization advanced, and the prairie chickens that thronged the wheat fields. Prairie chickens were plentiful in western North Dakota when Theodore Roosevelt was ranching there in the early eighteen eighties. He tells of a day when he and his brother, hunting with a pointer and a setter pup, drove from wheat field to wheat field in a buckboard, and finished their day

Shot was made by dropping small amounts of melted lead from the melting room at the top of a shot tower into a tank at the bottom, using the force of gravity to shape the pellets.

with 105 birds. John M. Murphy, an enthusiastic scattergunner of the late seventies, told of a day in the Kansas wheat fields when he and three companions bagged, despite a four-hour midday layoff, a grand total of ninety-three prairie chickens.

Those kills seem unduly large to present-day sportsmen, but at that time prairie chickens were so plentiful that it was not unusual for a farmer armed with an old muzzle-loading musket to kill, and sell, two or three thousand a year.

Western sportsmen also hunted the sage grouse, which lived on the dry plains and was as big as a young turkey. It was so unsuspicious that the frontiersmen called it the "fool hen." When it finally decided that it should leave the area, it labored into the air with a loud flapping of wings, then sailed away in steady flight. It was easy to hit, but could carry more lead than a ringneck pheasant and so was hard to kill. Its unsuspecting nature was its undoing, and it is now almost extinct.

On the Pacific Coast there were dusky grouse, and valley and mountain quail. Wild turkeys were abundant east of the Rockies—especially in the deep South, where some Negro hunters would build a blind, dig a trench in front of it, bait the trench with grain, and, when a flock walked into the trap, slaughter the big birds with muskets loaded almost to the muzzle. There were ruffed grouse and woodcock in New England thickets, waterfowl by the millions and quail aplenty in the stubble fields. It was during this bounteous time for wing-shooters, in the late eighteen seventies, that the breech-loading shotgun swept over America.

Our first breechloaders were either imported from England or assembled in America from English handmade barrels, locks, and actions. In either case they were far too costly for the average sportsman. And in America the average sportsman was all-important. Anyone who wanted to hunt had the right to do so, and

each year there were many thousands of new hunters in the field.

American firearms manufacturers, sensing the potential demand for a moderately priced shotgun, decided to apply to shotgun-making the same principle of mass production and interchangeable parts that had made their rifles the world's best. Within a few years gunmakers such as Daniel M. Lefever and his successive partners, Parker Brothers, the Ithaca Gun Company, and L. C. Smith were producing guns which lacked the hand finish and ornamentation of the high-priced English weapons but handled just as sweetly and shot as well. Colt, Stevens, Remington, Winchester, and other plants manufactured even lower-priced single- and double-barreled guns.

Barrels—made of iron or of a mixture of iron and steel—varied widely in quality. The first step in forging a barrel was to form a thin metal band called the ribbon. For a cheap barrel a single iron rod, twisted like a rope, was heated and hammered into a ribbon. For the so-called Damascus barrel, which was more expensive, from three to six rods of iron and steel were placed alternately side by side, their twists running in opposite directions, and flattened.

In either case the ribbon was coiled in a spiral around a mandrel, reheated, and the edges of the spiral welded together—an operation demanding great skill. The forging completed, the tube was reamed by a machine. Modern barrels are finished by bluing, but in those days they were browned—rusted a bit and polished. In the case of Damascus barrels, the acid used in the process had more effect on the softer iron than on the steel, leaving the steel fibers standing out in beautiful relief.

American firearms manufacturers and English gunsmiths raced to develop the hammerless gun. In 1866 the Whitney Arms Company (then run by a son of the Eli Whitney who had introduced the concept of interchangeable parts) produced a hammerless single-barreled gun operated by a lever action. In 1870 Murcott, a Britisher, made the first really good hammerless double-barreled gun. In 1876 Greener, a famous London gunsmith, exhibited a fine lever-cocking hammerless double at the Centennial Exposition in Philadelphia. Two years later Nicholas & Lefever marketed the first American hammerless double—a handsome weapon, cocked by a long side lever, which had been patented by "Uncle Dan" Lefever, one of the great names in American firearms making. The next year Clark & Sneider of Baltimore produced the first barrel-cocking hammerless double.

Another important innovation of this period was the Roper detachable choke—a thin steel sleeve inserted in the muzzle end of a shotgun bore. It was the forerunner of several effective variable-choke devices which now make one single-barreled gun serve different shooting needs.

American firearms manufacturers also developed the rotary bolt, the single trigger, the automatic ejector, and the ventilated rib; the machine-made shotguns they turned out were at least equal to the English handmade guns costing several times as much. With such weapons available, and feathered game still plentiful in many parts of the country, shotgunning became a truly national sport, and many men were happy to make long railroad journeys to enjoy a few days of better shooting than they could find close to home.

Trapshooting with live passenger pigeons as targets became popular in the eighteen seventies and for the next twenty years provided a profitable market for professional bird-netters. Several million passenger pigeons were sacrificed to this sport. Thirty-five thousand of them were bought for one big shoot in Oswego, New York, and ten thousand for a tournament at Coney Island—sponsored by the New York Association for the Protection of Fish and Game!

As a result of heavy gambling on the matches, guns and ammunition were some-times tampered with, and birds were cruelly mutilated to make them fly erratically when the trap was sprung. Public opinion turned strongly against live-bird shooting, and most states prohibited it in the early 1900s.

Captain Adam H. Bogardus had a much better idea. He was an ex-market hunter from Illinois who went to England and made good his claim to the world's championship by beating all the best British shots. It was great sports news, and he capitalized on it. He patented a trap which threw glass balls, and for a number of years traveled the country giving exhibitions of his skill in shattering these fragile "birds." On one occasion, he shot at 1,136 balls in 101 minutes, and broke 1,000 of them.

The manufacture of shotgun ammunition naturally became big business. Small powder mills grew into or were combined into big loading plants. Smokeless powder, introduced in shotgun ammunition in the eighteen eighties, increased the muzzle velocity of shot pellets from a thousand foot seconds to around twelve hundred with resultant increased killing power. It also made shooting a cleaner and more pleasant sport; in the old black-powder days it was standard practice for the quail hunter to shoot and then dive to the ground to try to mark his bird by floating feathers before the smoke curtain blinded him. The handsome old Damascus barrels, unable to withstand smokeless-powder pressures, were gradually replaced by precision-bored, plain steel tubes.

In 1883 there were six shot towers in the United States; together they made five thousand tons of shot a year. The highest and probably the oldest was the 246-foot Merchant's Shot Tower in Baltimore, Maryland, which was built more than a century ago and is still standing.

The force of gravity was the major factor in the making of shot. Pigs of lead hardened with arsenic or antimony were hoisted to the top of the tower where they were melted. Then the liquid metal was ladled into a perforated pan, suspended over an opening in the floor. The holes in the bottom of this outsize kitchen colander were slightly smaller than the size of the shot to be cast. The fine stream of metal lead pouring through the holes broke into pear-shaped drops which, as they continued to fall, became spherical. At the bottom of the tower they splashed into a tank of water, which did not distort them as would have happened if they had fallen on a hard surface.

The pellets were ladled from the tank, dried, then polished in a revolving cask containing a small amount of black lead. Then they were sent down a chute, where the perfectly round pellets gathered sufficient speed to jump a trough at the bottom while the slower-rolling imperfect ones fell into it. Finally, the good pellets were dropped through a series of graduated sieves which sorted them into different shot sizes.

Although more machinery is used in today's shot towers, gravity still does most of the work, and the fact that a ball will roll downhill remains the basic principle of the sorting operation.

At about the time smokeless powder was coming into use, American firearms manufacturers made their outstanding contribution to the shotgun's development—the repeater. The concept of a gun which would give the bird hunter more than two shots was neither new or untried, but the first successful repeat-

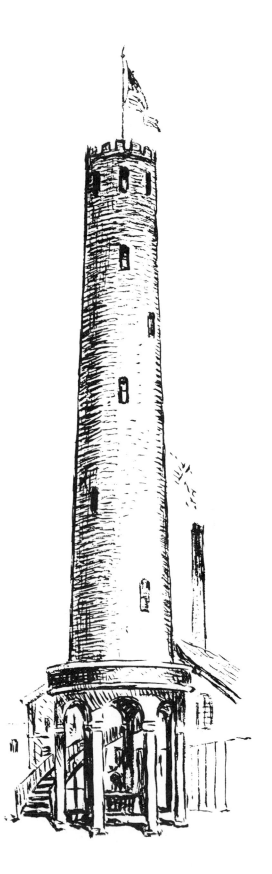

There were six shot towers in the United States in the eighteen eighties, producing five thousand tons of shot a year.

ing shotgun was the five-shot, tubular-magazine Spencer, brought out in 1882. The action was opened, the fired shell ejected, and a new shell loaded by a fore-end slide which was held in the left hand. An improved version, the Spencer-Roper, had a rather large sale. Winchester introduced its first repeating shotgun in 1887. A five-shot lever action much like the Model 1886 rifle, it was only moderately popular. In 1893 Winchester made its first pump gun; the Burgess Arms Company manufactured a repeater operated by a right-hand slide, or sleeve, fitting over the small of the stock; and Marlin produced a pump gun.

Four years later Winchester began to manufacture the Browning-designed Model 1897 five-shot, slide action, which was not discontinued until 1957. Browning was known as a designer of automatic pistols, machine guns, and other automatic weapons, but he ranks high among the developers of the repeating shotgun. In 1904 he designed the Stevens 520, the first hammerless repeater, and in 1915 the Remington Model 17 hammerless—both of them pump guns.

At about the time that Winchester brought out its Model 12 hammerless repeater, Browning also invented, in 1910, the recoil-operated autoloading shotgun which for many years was made in Belgium and, later, in this country.

With shotguns and their ammunition getting better and better, bag limits nonexistent or overlarge, market hunting a thriving business, and more sport hunters in the field each year, the upland game-bird population was drastically reduced through the eighteen-eighties and nineties. The real sportsmen of the country knew that something had to be done. Under the pressure of their public opinion, seasons were shortened, bag limits were cut, and the sale of wild game was made illegal. The pheasant, after becoming established in this country, provided good shooting for many thousands of hunters. Perhaps most important of all, the sportsman cold-shouldered the game hog and the man who shot his birds sitting. Shotgunning became what it should always be—a true sport, and a wonderful, challenging one.

CHAPTER 12

The Good Old Days of Waterfowling

Long before the moderate-priced, double-barreled, breech-loading shotgun was developed, waterfowling was a sport as well as a method of getting food. Scientists excavating the Lovelock Cave in Nevada some years ago unearthed duck decoys made of tule, a kind of large bulrush, which the Indians had made long before Columbus was born. All the early settlers in America went gunning for fowl, and some of them even practiced getting them on the wing. And by the middle eighteen fifties, market hunters operating within easy shipping distance of Baltimore, New York, Boston, and other Eastern cities were burning tons of black powder each spring and fall in their heavy six- and eight-gauge muzzle-loaders to satisfy the town dwellers' appetite for duck and wild goose meat. But even as late as the eighteen eighties the flights of canvasbacks, redheads, black ducks, scaup, pintails, Canada geese, black brant, and other waterfowl that shuttled between their immense breeding grounds in Canada and their wintering areas from Chesapeake Bay to Key West seemed inexhaustible.

Since the birds could be depended upon to be in well-known areas at definite times, waterfowling was the most profitable branch of market hunting, much of whose shameful story of greed and slaughter will be told in Chapter Thirteen. But even in the "good old days," before ducks and geese grew wary, getting a big bag every shooting day of the long open season was not always easy. The canvasback was as wily as it was fast; the black duck could "see a man as far as a man could see the moon"; and the old gander flying the Number One position in a string of snake-neck Canadas was never a fool. In the eighteen fifties, as now, successful waterfowling called for a good deal of experience and skill and patience.

The old market hunters had those qualities. They had their faults, but they were keen students of the birds on which their profits depended. Many sportsmen who took to waterfowl shooting learned the game from these highly competent professionals and adopted many of their ingenious and often devastating hunting methods.

As the observant Indians had known for centuries, most waterfowl winging through the air like to join a crowd of their kind which has apparently found a good feeding spot. The Indians turned this desire into duck meat by luring the birds within arrow-shooting distance with crude artificial decoys. White settlers achieved the same result through the old European custom of using live decoys—cripples which had recovered from their wounds but could not fly, or their wing-clipped descendants. The use of stool birds was undoubtedly known in early colonial times but did not become common until the days of large-scale market hunting.

In the East live decoys were used primarily in goose hunting. Professional gunners around Long Island's Shinnecock and Great South bays, who supplied the New York markets with waterfowl, did their shooting from coffin-like boxes sunk in the sand spits running out into the bay. The gunners reached their pits in scooters—duck skiffs equipped with steel runners, which could sail even better on ice than in water.

A decoy rig consisted of between fifteen and forty geese of both sexes, taken to the spit in coops. Stakes were driven into the sand at regular intervals and a bird was tethered to each stake by a leather leg strap or hobble. The most valuable member of the rig (worth up to two hundred dollars) was a trained gander tethered some distance from the other birds, so that its calls would attract wild geese passing overhead.

When the wild birds came down to the rig they mingled with and then separated from the stools. At that point the market hunters gave them two volleys—one while they were still on the ground or water and the other as they rose. At first, most sport gunners did the same, but in later years good sportsmanship usually prevailed and they shot their birds on the wing as they came in toward the stools.

On the Pacific Coast, and in many parts of the West, many goose kills were made by confining numbers of wing-clipped geese of different species in separate, wire-fenced enclosures within easy range of the nearby gunners' pits. But the art of decoying geese reached its height of deadly efficiency along the New England coast, where the stool birds were trained—with corn and endless patience—to fly out to meet flocks of their wild kin and lure them to the blinds.

Live decoys were not used extensively in Eastern duck shooting, although some gunners found that a few birds swimming among wooden stools added a touch of animation and naturalness to the rig that might bring in even the canny redheads and canvasbacks. In the Middle West—especially in Missouri and Arkansas, where the mallard is the most prized duck—nearly all market hunters and many sportsmen had a number of noisy, wing-clipped greenheads, which often were so well trained that they would hop aboard the skiff when the hunter called them at the time to start home.

The use of live decoys was banned by federal regulation in the depth of the duck depression of the middle nineteen thirties. Many veteran waterfowl hunters still regret the change, saying that much of the charm and interest of wildfowl shooting is gone. The man who owned a drake and half a dozen Susies often grew as fond of them as his dog, and was thrilled to watch them lure their wild relatives down to the guns.

The artificial decoy, which is now used almost the world over for sport, was a purely American innovation. The first settlers no doubt got the idea from the Indians, who never used live decoys. Although we now know that at least one tribe made creditable floating duck decoys many centuries ago, most Indians were satisfied with improvised lures —lumps of mud protruding from shallow water (they still tempt mallards, pintails, and teal within range of hidden guns on the Utah marshes), dead birds propped or anchored in more or less realistic poses, or perhaps a duck skin with the feathers left on and stuffed with dry grass.

The earliest artificial decoys made by white men were stick-ups—bird profiles whittled from a pine board, painted or decorated with real wings, and supported by sticks thrust into the mud. They were much used in early snipe shooting, and some of them were so realistic that they drew fire from novice sportsmen. Profile goose decoys are used even now—notably in Western wheat fields and on the Mississippi River sand bars.

Stick-ups, however, can be used only on land or in very shallow water. Because of the large numbers of canvasbacks and other choice "dollar ducks" lying well offshore in the coastal bays, often in rough water, it was natural that floating decoys would be developed. It seems likely that these were first used on Great South Bay before the Revolution. At any rate, they were in fairly general use along the coast in the early eighteen hundreds.

The professionals, finding that large rigs of live decoys were difficult to handle in deep water, were quick to appreciate the many advantages of the artificial floating decoys which they called stools, tollers, or blocks. They were easily carried in a duck skiff; they were rugged

enough to stand rough and long use; they did not have to be fed; and they were very successful in attracting ducks within shooting range.

Many market hunters made their own decoys, during the off season when the birds were somewhere else. Working at a chopping block with a carpenter's hatchet, it didn't take a man long to hew a lifelike decoy from a piece of white cedar or white pine, and to smooth it down with a drawknife and sandpaper. A talented whittler—and most Americans were good whittlers in those days—could carve out

Bushwacking was productive on the Susquehanna Flats, near Havre de Grace, Maryland, where hunters sculled swan-shaped boats toward the unsuspecting ducks.

thirty or forty heads in a day. The painting was usually crude, but the completed product did its appointed task. Some of today's high-priced decoys are real works of art, but they cannot fool a duck any more completely than did those that baymen used to sell for a quarter or half-dollar each.

Shortly after the Civil War, when the commercial demand for ducks became strong and the use of decoys was spreading from the Atlantic Coast to other sections of the country, several business firms started to turn them out by machine. Professionals and seasoned sportsmen were inclined to be scornful of these "gunstore decoys," but during the next forty years several million were sold, at prices ranging from two dollars and fifty cents to twelve dollars a dozen. In the South and West they played an important part in the disgraceful nationwide slaughter of waterfowl.

Sportsmen of this day of comparatively few ducks and many restrictions on shooting them look back to that Golden Age with mingled envy and disgust. For more than half a century America had better waterfowl shooting than any other country. From a conservation standpoint the near-destruction of a priceless natural resource belonging to all the people was revolting; and the horde of greedy market hunters was abetted in this destruction, all too often, by game hogs calling themselves sportsmen and lacking even the weak excuse that they killed to earn a living.

Along the Atlantic Coast battery shooting —especially of the high-priced canvasback and redheads—was the principal method used. It started on Long Island bays, and apparently no one even tried to enforce a state law which had been passed in 1838 prohibiting it.

Far out on the wide bays the ducks were less wary than when flying close to the land, and unless they saw a boat near by they came unsuspectingly close to the large rigs of bobbing blocks on the water. The gunner's big problem was to stay within shooting distance of his stools. This he accomplished by using a battery or sinkbox—probably the most dangerous and uncomfortable craft ever designed, but highly effective for its purpose.

A typical single battery was about twelve feet long and seven feet wide. Its body was a shallow, narrow-decked "coffin" just large enough for a gunner to lie down in. Wings built of canvas over wood ribs extended from the deck. The cockpit coaming was made of sheet lead which could be bent up to keep out the wash on rough days. Everything was painted marsh-green. After the battery had been anchored within range of the stools, a number of twenty-pound cast-iron duck decoys were placed on the wings; these plus the weight of the gunner brought the deck almost flush with the water.

A helper in a skiff or dory lay well downwind off the rig, to pick up dead birds and finish off the cripples. If a sudden wind came up and the helper could not reach the sinkbox, the gunner threw his iron ducks overboard, cut the anchor rope, and drifted or poled downwind. Usually he managed to reach land, but battery shooting resulted in numerous drownings.

If battery shooting was sometimes dangerous, it was always uncomfortable. The gunner lay on his back, usually blown by a knifelike wind and splashed with icy spray, with only his eyes and the top of his head above the coaming. The ducks never seemed to notice the sinkbox, but if the gunner raised his head too soon they sailed away. So when he saw birds flying toward his rig he had to keep his patience until they set their wings and reached for the water with their legs. Then he sat up and shot. After the city sportsman had undergone this ordeal a few dozen times, he began to suspect that there must be better ways to get waterfowl.

Sinkbox shooting was a rugged form of sport, but it had its redeeming points, as any pre-1935 salt-water duck hunter will verify.

It too was banned because it resulted in too many dead birds. Professionals on North Carolina's Currituck Sound, Virginia's Back Bay, and spots farther north used batteries and sometimes as many as five hundred decoys to make huge kills of canvasbacks, redheads, and other ducks.

Probably the worst one-day slaughter was perpetrated by three Long Island market hunters in December, 1898. Starting to shoot at daybreak, and spelling one another so that there were always two gunners in the double sinkbox, they killed 640 ducks, most of them broadbills. Even more astounding was the murderous performance of a professional near Havre de Grace, Maryland. On opening day of the 1879 season he shot alone from a sinkbox on the Susquehanna Flats. One of his two 10-gauge, double-barreled shotguns burst early in the morning. He continued to shoot with the other, dousing it in the water when it became too hot to handle. Before darkness forced him to stop, he had killed 509 canvasbacks and redheads.

Battery shooting was deadly on ducks, but other methods devised by market hunters and adopted by many sportsmen were almost as effective. Bushwhacking, for example, was highly productive on the famous Susquehanna Flats. The boats used—just large enough to carry a gunner and a man who worked a sculling oar through a hole in the stern—were built in the form of huge swans. Accompanied by a number of floating decoys, one of these odd craft was gently sculled within range of a band of ducks. They watched its approach with unalarmed curiosity—until the gunner opened fire.

Along the shores of Chesapeake Bay a hundred years or more ago, some waterfowl hunters used "tollers"—dogs trained to cut capers with a stick or handkerchief. The intense curiosity of the ducks brought them within range of hidden gunners. Dogs so trained are still used for this kind of shooting in Nova Scotia.

Shooting from brush blinds built on points or sand spits, or on piles out in the open water, with rigs set out to attract the birds, was a popular and rewarding form of hunting. On New Jersey's Barnegat Bay, shooting from the well-known Barnegat sneakboxes over stools of hollow decoys, called dugouts, resulted in big bags of game for both sportsmen and mar-

Shore-bird gunners on the Maryland marshes wore high hats, not for style but so other hunters could see them over the reeds.

ket hunters. In 1899 one old bayman, shooting an ancient 8-gauge muzzle-loader, killed 115 ducks in a day, and could have killed more if he had not run out of powder.

Shore-bird shooting was very popular. At one time there were so many poling boats working the narrow thoroughfares of Maryland's Patuxent River marshes that the gunners had to wear old high hats so that other hunters would recognize them as human beings and refrain from peppering them. A less pleasing anecdote relates the performance of some members of a Chesapeake Bay duck club who used to shoot their limit of two hundred shore birds, day after day, and leave them to rot where they fell.

Waterfowling spread westward from the Atlantic Coast and became a national sport. At the same time, commercialized waterfowl slaughter became a national disgrace. There was good shooting almost everywhere. In the early eighteen eighties, Theodore Roosevelt, out for meat for his Dakota ranch hands, got eleven teal on the water with his first shotgun barrel and a pair of shovelers in the air with his second; another time he and a companion killed forty-three ducks in the course of one day's hunting.

There was wonderful goose and duck shooting in the wheat fields of the prairie provinces. Pass-shooting mallards from a cranky double-ender skiff in the timber holes of the flooded bottoms of the Illinois River, or on the White River bottoms in Arkansas, was as fine scattergun sport as could be found anywhere in the world. A Missouri gunner who called himself a sportsman bragged of having killed 350 ducks in a day. On the Iowa-Minnesota border a competent market hunter could—and often did—kill three thousand bluewing teal, mallards, and bluebills in a season. Everywhere ducks and geese were shot down by the thousands.

For both the sportsman and the market hunter that abundant and unrestricted age of American waterfowl shooting was glorious,

while it lasted. But it could not last forever. The market hunters began to realize this, and became very reticent about the number of birds they killed in a season. Around 1890 a few sportsmen with a concern for the future recognized as a danger signal the fact that each year there were fewer birds than there had been the year before. They urged restrictive measures, but most of the state lawmakers, vote-conscious and believing the conservationists to be only a small minority, declined to reduce bag limits; they seemed to feel that the best time to close the season was when the ducks were somewhere else than in in their state.

Among those who saw the need for federal regulation was the late George Shiras, III, pioneer wildlife photographer. In 1904, as a member of Congress, he introduced the first migratory bird bill, but it was not enacted into law until 1913. Its essential provisions were incorporated in the Migratory Bird Treaty with Great Britain, which became effective in 1918. By prohibiting spring shooting and banning the sale of game, it put the market hunters out of business.

These restrictions, combined with the light hunting during the first World War, resulted in a waterfowl comeback, but the gain was soon canceled out. By 1935 the waterfowl population had dropped to an all-time low of an estimated twenty-seven million, largely because of a tremendous postwar increase in the number of hunters and a record-breaking drought. In this crisis, the federal authorities shortened seasons, drastically reduced bag limits, and prohibited battery shooting.

Greedy "sportsmen" certainly aided the market hunters in ending forever the great days of waterfowling, but the latter must take most of the blame, for they were more thorough and businesslike in their undertakings. While they were permitted to operate, the market hunters dealt just as efficiently with other birds and all kinds of game animals as they did with waterfowl.

CHAPTER 13

How Market Hunters Massacred the Game

Killing game and selling it was a traditional and legitimate way of earning a living during the early days of America. But severe and sometimes irreparable damage to our wildlife resulted because we permitted the practice to continue long after our need for it.

Most of the first settlers hunted for themselves. As the settlements grew, a few men who liked life in the wilds made a business of hunting game and selling their kill to town dwellers. Some of them, such as Daniel Boone and his fictional counterpart, Fenimore Cooper's Natty Bumppo, became picturesque figures in our early history, legend, and literature. Without these buckskin-clothed specialists and the game they hunted, the course of American history might have been different. Certainly civilization's march across the continent would have been slower, for it was the professional hunters who, on many successive frontiers, supplied the meat for the men of other occupations who transformed a wilderness into a great nation.

As long as these hunters killed game only to supply isolated settlements with fresh meat, their killing—heavy as it was—was justified. But conditions changed when the railroads caught up with the frontier. Beef and pork

being easily obtainable (and preferred by the frontiersmen), game meat was no longer an essential food. The sale of game should have been stopped then. It was not stopped because no one realized that game is one of our renewable natural resources. Some men believed that the supply of animals and birds was inexhaustible. Others thought that all game had to disappear when the country became completely settled. Both were wrong, so the slaughter continued.

Frank Mayer, the buffalo hunter who has been mentioned in preceding chapters, was one of the last of the professionals who killed game to supply areas not yet reached by the railroads. In 1878, when buffaloes were so scarce that hunting them was no longer very profitable, Mayer went to Colorado to prospect for gold. He found Leadville a typical boom town jammed with fifteen thousand people competing for food and lodging. Meat was especially scarce; tough beef cost a dollar and fifty cents a pound when it was available.

Mayer, who had a good business head, contracted to furnish a wholesaler every week with at least three tons of big game, rough-dressed. He was to be paid ten cents a pound for deer, elk, and antelope; twelve and a half

cents for mountain sheep; and fifteen cents for bear. A freighter agreed, for a fifty per cent cut of the proceeds, to send out a twelve-horse team once a week and haul the kill into Leadville.

With a combination cook and handyman, Mayer set up his camp in the high country near the Blue River. His armament consisted of three single-shot rifles—his favorite .40/70 Sharps, a .40/90 Ballard, and a .45/70 Sharps. In these guns Mayer was able to use home-made, hollow-nose bullets.

Early on his first morning of hunting, Mayer got two mule deer in line and broke their necks with a single bullet. He worked a couple of timbered arroyos and killed six more deer with ten shots. Then he scored clean kills on three running mule deer at fairly long ranges. He had eleven deer the first morning—not sensational shooting for the West of the eighteen seventies, but an encouraging start.

In the afternoon Mayer switched to the Ballard, knocked over two antelope with the same bullet, and brought off a couple of running shots at four hundred yards. He estimated the day's kill at twenty-six hundred pounds.

The next day he killed three bull elk and four cows that rough-dressed at more than three thousand pounds. In two days of hunting he had killed his week's quota of about three tons. His second week's bag was eight elk and a dozen deer that added up to seventy-five hundred pounds of meat—and he used only twenty cartridges for the entire job!

Geese, driven from
roosts by bonfires, were
ruthlessly harvested
and sent to market.

Mountain sheep were the hunter's most interesting but least profitable quarry. Climbing after them was the hardest kind of work, and they were wary and difficult to stalk. But one morning Mayer got five mountain sheep in not many more minutes. In addition he bagged, that week, twenty-four deer, nine elk, and a grizzly bear. In three weeks of hunting he killed more than fourteen tons of game. His half of the proceeds was $1,422.

Like Mayer, all professional hunters of the frontier killed mercilessly to meet the needs of the towns they supplied with meat. Because lack of transportation restricted their hunting to areas close to those towns, the damage they did to our big game was localized. They never bothered with game birds or waterfowl except for their own pots.

The railroad lines made market hunting unnecessary, as has been pointed out, but they also made it more profitable, because they could carry game long distances to the big cities. Soon the game areas were overrun by a horde of greedy, full-time and part-time market hunters eager to cash in on this larger market. There were several types of market hunters. The best of them was neither angel nor devil. Most of them were unskilled and too lazy to make much profit, but there were so many of these that they probably killed at least as much game as the more competent and industrious professionals did. There were also many thousands of farmers who shot or trapped game birds for the market. And there were many men and boys who made occasional destructive raids on any game that was easy to kill and not too far away.

The whitetail deer was profitable prey for Eastern market hunters and those in the Great Lakes region. In northern Michigan in the late eighteen seventies and through the eighteen eighties, a competent hunter could kill from 150 to 200 whitetails in the autumn, and get between fifteen and twenty dollars for each of them. This added up to more money than the average lumberjack, farmer, or miner could earn by twelve months of hard work. So it is not surprising that hunters killed deer industriously all through the long open season and often before and after it. In daylight they stillhunted with the rifle. After dark they jacklighted blazed trails around swamps and along ridges with bull's-eye lanterns fastened to their caps or on poles strapped to their backs and extending above their heads. When the gleam of a deer's eyes showed in the light's beam, the whitetail was an easy mark with a buckshot-loaded scattergun. Other jacklighters patrolled the shores of lakes and streams in canoes; often their kills were does or fawns.

Night and day, week after week, this killing went on. It has been estimated that in the early eighteen eighties market hunters bagged most of the eighty thousand deer that were killed in Michigan each fall. After the whitetails had been thinned out by years of such hunting, men had to go farther to make their kills, and much of the meat was wasted. When a deer was shot deep in the woods, often only its saddle was packed out to the railroad.

Sportsmen finally got the season in Michigan shortened from four months to one in 1887. Seven years later they persuaded the legislature to pass a license law and impose a season limit of five deer. But the law did little good. Market hunters took out licenses in the names of relatives and friends; they did not, it is true, kill quite so many deer that next season, but they were better off because the restrictions had forced up the price of venison. Not until the season limit was reduced to one buck and the sale of venison made illegal could market hunting for deer be stopped.

In neighboring Wisconsin, market hunters had to be content with a smaller take. There is a record of four thousand whitetails having been shipped out of the town of Antigo in four months in the early eighteen eighties, but that was unusual. One party of three good hunters who worked together for many years were well satisfied with one hundred deer a season.

Some hunters hired out to kill whitetails for the logging camps, but this could never mean a serious drain on the deer because lumberjacks were beefeaters who roared their disapproval if venison appeared on the table too frequently.

Most of the deer killed by the Great Lakes-area market hunters went to the big Midwestern cities for the luxury trade. Game dealers in New York and other Eastern cities got most of their venison from Maine and the Adirondacks where, although the kills were heavy, market hunting never reached the scale it did in Michigan.

The most complete and the most shocking of the many crimes against our game was the extinction of the passenger pigeon. From earliest colonial times until long after the Civil War, millions of these fast-flying birds migrated each year. In 1857 the Ohio legislature replied to pleas for their protection with the statement: "The passenger pigeon needs no protection . . . no ordinary destruction can lessen them." In 1871 *one* nesting area in Wisconsin covered 850 square miles of woodlands and was estimated at 136,000,000 birds. As late as 1878 a nesting area in Michigan covered 150,000 acres and was populated by an estimated billion and a half pigeons.

The last passenger pigeon died in a Cincinnati zoo in 1914.

Although market hunters are rightly blamed for the extermination of this excellent game bird, the professional shotgun hunters played only a small part in it. The pigeons could be bagged easily by other methods, and the price they brought did not justify much expenditure of powder and shot. The slaughter was instigated by market buyers and carried out by gangs of killers assisted by thousands of men and boys eager to cash in on a few days or nights of bloody work.

Now-extinct passenger pigeons were released from cages and shot by trapshooters. Millions were slaughtered in this way before the "sport" was finally outlawed.

Netting was the favorite method of catching passenger pigeons. An appropriate opening in the woods was selected, the ground was baited with salt, and a few stool pigeons were planted—birds blinded by having their eyes sewed shut. A large net was rigged high overhead. The birds came to the bait eagerly and when they blanketed the ground two or three deep the net was dropped. The pigeons were either killed for the market or crated alive for sale to trapshooting clubs. A single cast netted five hundred to a thousand birds, and a dozen casts a day was not unusual.

Other pigeon killers beat the roosting birds out of trees with poles and clubs. After dark, big fires were lighted, and in their glare the massacre went on all night. When the squabs were old enough to send to market, the nests were knocked out of trees.

The killings reached astronomical figures. In one month in 1878, almost fifteen million pigeons were shipped to market from the one Michigan town of Petoskey, and it is estimated that in that year more than a billion wild pigeons were sold in the United States. Market buyers, provided with barrels and ice, often accompanied the killers and bought their take. Sometimes so many pigeons were sent to market that the price broke and the birds sold for a penny each retail.

It is remarkable that the passenger pigeons lasted as long as they did. Their breeding rate was the lowest of any game bird, since the hens laid only one or two eggs at a time, and it was thought that they nested only once a year. In most parts of the country their decline was gradual; there were fewer and smaller flights each year until they were gone. In some areas they disappeared with dramatic suddenness.

Most successful of all the men who made game-killing their trade was H. Clay Merritt. He built a sizable business from a few charges of powder and shot, and was chiefly responsible for the disappearance of game birds from several large Midwestern areas.

Merritt was born in 1831 on a farm near Carmel, New York, on the route of the market wagons which rumbled by with loads of game for New York City, fifty miles away. He had a gun before he was ten. When he went to Williams College, in Massachusetts, he kept his landlady's boarding-house table supplied with ruffed grouse. In the late summers, when he was at home, he shot woodcock and grouse which he sold in a nearby resort town. After graduating from college he taught school for a year and shot for the market in his spare time. One day a game buyer said to him, "You're a good hunter. Why don't you go out to Illinois, where there's enough game to make hunting worth while?" Merritt liked shooting better than teaching school, and he had two uncles in Henry County, Illinois. He went there in the summer of 1855.

Henry County was a dreary place about 150 miles west of Chicago. There were few settlements, the roads were bad, most of the trees that stood were fire-scarred, and prairie farms were unfenced and mostly untilled because the railroad was too far away to take crops to market. But Henry County was a bird hunter's paradise. There were prairie chickens everywhere, quail in the fields, golden plover in the thickets, and snipe and mallards in the river bottoms. In the towns, woodcock fed in the yards, quail roamed the streets, and housewives used their brooms to chase grouse outdoors.

Merritt could have killed five hundred birds a week, but there was no market for them until 1858, when a railroad was built through Henry County. Then he really started to hunt. The shooting was easy; with a muzzle-loader he could kill a hundred plover in a morning, and as many prairie chickens, or sixty or seventy snipe in a full day. He estimated that each year for thirty years twenty-five thousand jacksnipe were killed for the market in Illinois. The demand for quail was so great that he hired several men to join in the shooting.

He hunted woodcock, prairie chickens, quail, snipe and ducks in Henry County for several years, now, and then crossing the Mississippi into Iowa and killing more game there. He soon had a gang of hunters working through the season, and each year he shipped about five tons of birds to game dealers in New York City's Washington Market.

Merritt switched to the breechloader when it came into use, and each autumn he bought a new 10-gauge double-barreled gun. He hunted so much that if he used a gun more than one season, its barrels became leaded. In 1867 he had a small paddle-wheel steamboat built, and for six years used it on the upper Mississippi as a mobile camp for himself and a dozen hired hunters. He shipped the game by railroad from the river towns. In 1870 he installed a refrigeration plant at his Henry County headquarters and held game until prices were high.

When he stopped shooting three years later, Henry County and all the land within easy reach of it had been practically stripped of game birds, almost entirely because of his activities. But there were still plenty of birds beyond the Missouri, so he sent his son there to shoot them and to buy them. He continued to manage his extensive business until 1893, when the growing prohibitions on the sale of game made it unprofitable. He retired a wealthy man.

Merritt was typical of thousands of men all over America who made a business of killing, and who profited at the expense of sportsmen by taking far more than their fair share of the game. How much upland game they killed no one knows. An indication of the size of the slaughter may be gained from a fact-based estimate, made in the eighteen seventies, that in Iowa alone a million prairie chickens were killed each season during a period of several years.

All the birds did not fall to the guns. Trapping was even more devastating to some species. Many Midwestern farmers trapped a thousand prairie chickens a week in snowy weather. Two Massachusetts men, in the early eighteen eighties, snared and sold four hundred ruffed grouse a month. There is also a record of two New York market hunters who shot one thousand grouse in a single season in the late eighties. This game bird was so popular with epicures that some of the fine hotels hired their own grouse hunters.

Even robins and other now-protected songbirds were sacrificed to satisfy the profitable demand. In Texas a party of hunters bagged 10,157 robins. Residents of one town in Louisiana killed 120,000 and sold them for five cents a dozen. The junco was recommended for convalescents. Housewives bought mixed strings of purple finches, meadow larks, and catbirds; they baked pies of goldfinches and cedar waxwings. The Eskimo curlew was so abundant that Midwestern hunters killed as many at 2,500 a day. Around Omaha, Nebraska, in the early seventies, market hunters frequently dumped carloads by the roadside when the price fell.

The heath hen, now extinct, was once a drug on the market in New York City. The dowitcher was among the delicacies that could command a good price in Chicago. Entire flocks of greater or lesser yellowlegs were wiped out. A list of birds once available at New York City markets includes bobolinks, grouse, swans, loons, wild turkeys, pheasants, partridges, snipe, plover, sandpipers, curlews, seaside finches, skylarks, meadow larks, wood tattlers, orioles, snow buntings, blackbirds, kingfishers, blue jays, brown thrashers, thrushes, and bullfinches.

In Chapter Twelve we saw a few of the effects of market hunting on waterfowl populations. Ducks were usually more profitable than grouse or quail, so many hunters concentrated on them. Ducks were so plentiful in many parts of the country during the eighties that a good shot who was also moderately industrious could kill three thousand in a season. A hunter could hire out to some market-supplying outfit for seventy-five dollars a month plus keep—good wages for that time.

In many places in the Midwest and on the Pacific Coast there were so many geese that they were a menace to agriculture. Naturally, the farmers gladly permitted market hunters to kill them off, which they did in many ingenious ways. They approached the geese under cover of a horse or an ox, and at close range blasted with huge smoothbores, knocking over from ten to forty at each discharge. Fire hunting was another method. A roosting ground was located, and after dark several large piles of dry wood were lighted. The geese, terrified but attracted by the glare, rose from their roosts and hovered over the fires until hundreds had been shot down.

Ducks, however, were the most profitable birds for the market hunters. One noted professional, Captain Theodore Johnson, killed a hundred thousand waterfowl in the decade he worked the bayous and swamps of the Mississippi delta below New Orleans. He considered 150 birds an average day's bag; in the

A housewife could buy songbirds, waterfowl, or upland game in the markets.

biggest week of his colorful career he killed more than a thousand.

Johnson sent his birds to the New Orleans markets. Greenwing teal, mallards, and pintails brought as much as eighty or as little as twenty-two and a half cents a pair. Shovelers, gadwalls, and pigeons were "trash ducks" for which he was lucky to get fifteen cents a pair. Johnson loved hunting, although he did not make a fortune out of it, and when a bag limit was imposed in 1911 he quit and became a guide.

Even before that date most market hunting in the United States had become either illegal or unprofitable. But even now, half a century later, we are still paying for the looting of one of our greatest recreational resources. We are paying for it in game shortages, brief open seasons, and skimpy bag limits. These restrictions are our heritage from the market hunters.

CHAPTER 14

The War Against the Predators

owboys riding slow circles through the night around the resting herds used to sing reassuringly:

Oh, lay still, dogies, since you have laid
down;
Stretch away out on the big open ground;
Snore loud, little dogies, and drown the
  wild sound
That will all go away when the day rolls
  'round—
Hi-oo, hi-oo, oo-oo.

The wild sound that the night guards crooned about to their apprehensive charges was the weird howling of packs of wolves that menaced the cattle. There were other wilderness killers, too—mountain lions, bears, bobcats, and coyotes—that trailed the herds wherever they went.

Some of those predators are no longer much of a threat, but there is still the puma—called the mountain lion in the Rocky Mountains, the cougar in the Pacific Northwest, and the panther, painter, or catamount in the East and South. One night, only thirty years ago, a puma got into a flock of ewes in western Colorado and methodically killed 192.

Halfway measures are useless in dealing with the puma. Man and the big, sleek, handsome cat cannot get along together, and one or the other must move out of an area when they meet. In earlier days in the West it was not always the puma that had to move. Its natural prey is the deer, but, as many ranchmen learned to their sorrow, it soon grows so fond of beef or mutton that raising cattle becomes a precarious business in puma country.

Another appetite of the puma's makes it impossible for the animal to get along with man. It has a keen taste for horseflesh and has been known to transform itself from the hunted to the hunter in order to satisfy that hunger. One such puma gave a government predator-hunter the most thrilling quarter-hour of his exciting career. His hounds had been tracking the animal for several hours. Finally the trail led into a canyon where the going was so rough that the hunter tied his horse to a tree and continued on foot behind his dogs. He glanced up and saw a puma creeping along the rim of the canyon toward the place where he had left his mount. It was the very cat he was after, doubling back on higher ground, with the hounds in pursuit. They were rapidly overtaking the puma as the hunter ran back down the canyon, but they were not fast enough. Just as the man met his dogs and closed in, the puma sprang onto the back of his terrified, plunging horse—but his attack and his career were ended abruptly by a bullet from the hunter's .30/30 rifle.

In the early days panthers caused a great deal of trouble for Eastern and Southern settlers, but they were gradually eliminated by hunters such as Meshach Browning, who killed more than fifty in the forty-four years he spent in the mountains of western Maryland. By 1880 they were almost exterminated east of the Mississippi. But for many years after that they remained a serious menace in many parts of the West. They were so adept at keeping out of sight that only a few were killed in chance encounters with sportsmen or cowhands, and the stockmen had to hire professional hunters to rid the range of them.

One of the most famous of those hunters was John B. Goff who killed three hundred pumas between 1885 and 1900, most of them in the rough country north of the White River in northwestern Colorado. He used foxhounds to trail his quarry, and mongrel fighting dogs to hold it at bay until he could kill it. In 1901 Theodore Roosevelt, then Vice President, went hunting with him in 20-below-zero weather. They were out five weeks and killed fourteen pumas, the largest weighing 227 pounds.

On one hunt, Roosevelt narrowly escaped getting hurt badly. The hounds had brought an old female puma to bay. Three of the fighting dogs had it by the head, so impulsive T. R., his sixgun in his left hand and a long hunting knife in his right, leaped in to make the kill. But at that moment the puma wrenched its head free and turned on him. One of the dogs got a fresh grip on the cat's paw. Roosevelt jammed his revolver butt between the puma's snapping jaws and, as the sharp teeth crunched down on it, killed the animal with a knife thrust between its shoulders.

The puma is the most unpredictable of all our predators. It is usually so shy that hunters in country where it is plentiful may go for weeks without seeing one. But at other times it shows no fear of men. There are numerous well-authenticated stories of its tracking men for long distances, apparently out of simple curiosity; in a few instances it has gone out of its way to attack them.

Another evidence of its unpredictability is its varying reaction to dogs. Although it often weighs more than two hundred pounds and its heavy paws are armed with long claws that have a terrible ripping power, it will sometimes let a single wirehaired terrier run it up a

Theodore Roosevelt narrowly escaped injury in 1901 when a female puma suddenly wrenched free of his dogs and lunged at him.

tree and keep it there. Giles Goswick, who in his twenty-seven years as a government hunter has killed 352 mountain lions, hasn't had a hound killed by one of them. Yet sometimes one of the big long-tailed cats will elect to fight to the finish with a pack of hounds, and may kill several of them before the hunter can get in a finishing shot.

The man who probably possessed the greatest fund of first-hand knowledge about the ways of the puma was the late Ben Lilly, who for years worked as a predator killer for stockmen over much of the West and who late in life became a government hunter. Although he lost count before he died, many Westerners credit him with killing more mountain lions than any other hunter. He developed a profound admiration for his prey's intelligence. "If you follow a lion for four or five days and don't get some education," he once told a fellow hunter, "you had better go back to plowing."

By 1915, predators were killing perhaps half a million calves, sheep, and colts a year, and great numbers of game animals in addition. In that year Congress responded to the pleas of stock raisers and sportsmen by making an appropriation for predator control under the U. S. Bureau of Biological Survey—now the Fish and Wildlife Service. Behind that long-overdue action by the federal lawmakers was almost half a century of persistent, costly, and largely unsuccessful effort by the stockmen to "kill their own snakes."

From the beginning of the exploration of the West predatory animals had been a nuisance to travelers and settlers alike. In the middle eighteen seventies changed conditions transformed these gangsters of the wild from an expensive nuisance to a grim menace.

In 1864 Sam Hartsel drove a herd of shorthorns across the Plains from Missouri to Colorado, and proved that the remarkably succulent prairie grasses made it possible for cattle to survive the blizzard-whipped winters of the high range. The news of his success spread fast. When the Civil War ended, hundreds of thousands of shorthorns from east of the Missouri and longhorns from Texas were driven into the immense Great Plains country, to graze unfenced within sight of the dwindling buffalo herds.

The wolves, pumas, and other predators, more than normally ravenous because merciless commercialized hunting had drastically depleted the hoofed game that was their natural prey, turned to the cattle for food, and to the sheep which soon shared the range. In self-defense the stockmen declared war to the death on predators. Some outfits imported packs of hounds to hunt them down, and every cowhand riding the range had orders to kill every predator he could with lead or poison. But immense hordes of killers still skulked around the herds and flocks. Predator-killing was apparently a full-time job for specialists, so the stockmen tried to make it a profitable job by offering bounties. But the number of predators kept increasing. Bounties reached an all-time high in the early nineteen hundreds, when a stockmen's association in Colorado offered $150 for killing an adult wolf. Bill Caywood, an expert trapper who later became a noted government hunter, moved in and within a year earned for himself a nice home ranch by killing 140 wolves, adults and whelps.

However, the bounty system had a serious weakness. Hunters and trappers found it very profitable to eliminate the more easily killed predators, but not the smarter ones whose liquidation demanded weeks or even months of persistent hard work. The inevitable result was that bounty hunters always left enough predator seed-stock to reinfest the district.

Officials of the Bureau of Biological Survey had made careful plans to cope with the predator problem, and as soon as Congress gave the necessary funds, they went into action. Experienced hunters and trappers were hired at decent salaries, but—to make certain that the craftiest predators would be run down— they could not accept bounties, and the pelts they took belonged to the government. That regulation is no longer in effect.

Most of the early government hunters were as colorful as they were competent. Typical of them was the previously mentioned Ben Lilly, "last of the mountain men." He was more than seventy when he pinned the federal bronze shield on his shirt, but he could still walk down a puma or a bear and score one-shot kills when his hounds cornered his prey. Most people who knew him thought that he was a bit "teched in the head" from years of solitary liv-

ing, for he talked to the animals he hunted and claimed that they talked to him. He admired and respected bears and mountain lions, but he had an insatiable desire to hunt them.

In 1936 Mrs. Bess Kennedy became the first woman to wear the bronze shield of the government predator hunter and trapper. A town-bred girl who loved dancing and parties, at the age of sixteen she married a ranchman who later turned government hunter. The first night she spent on the range the howling of the coyotes frightened her so badly that she wanted to go home. But she learned to ride, shoot, and trap, and in her years as a government hunter she has bagged her full share of mountain lions and held her own with the best

Traveling on skis and camouflaged in white, government hunters became expert wolf trackers.

of the men in the day-by-day trapping of coyotes and bobcats.

An earlier chapter has told of the battle against the grizzly bear, one of the most dangerous tasks that early Western settlers had to tackle. Although comparatively few grizzlies preyed on cattle or sheep, the occasional killer gave ranchmen a great deal of trouble. Once it had broken the neck of a cow with one cuff of its huge paw, it was "spoilt" and kept on attacking stock since it was such an easy way to get food.

A few well-to-do stockmen combined sport with business by hunting stock-killing grizzlies with dogs. The most successful of these was probably Montague Stevens, a British aristocrat turned New Mexico ranchman, who between 1893 and 1908 killed many of them, including several weighing eight hundred pounds, with his pack of purebred bloodhounds. But a more common method of eliminating "spoilt" bears was to take advantage of their habit of returning to feed on their kills and to shoot them from nearby cover. In this chore the ranchmen had the enthusiastic cooperation of many eager sportsmen. One of them was Henry L. Stimson, cabinet officer under three Presidents. He had a special .75-caliber, single-shot Winchester rifle with which, in his younger years, he scored a number of one-shot kills.

By the time the government undertook predator control, persistent hunting had driven most of the grizzlies deep into wilderness areas where they do man little harm. But numerous black bears, which had become notorious stock killers, remained to be tracked down.

Giles Goswick enjoyed this work as much as he did reducing the puma population, but on one of his hunts he got into trouble. His hounds were running a six-hundred-pound black bear up the bank of a creek, and from the noise they were making around a bend just ahead he was sure they had the animal at bay.

He hurried on and found the yelping dogs clustered around the mouth of a cave. When Giles drew close the bear came out, scattered the hounds, and charged straight at him. A hasty shot staggered the bear, but before Giles could lever another shell into the chamber it stumbled back into the cave.

Giles's job was to kill that bear. He coaxed one of his hounds to go into the cave, and he followed it. There was not a sound from the dog as the tunnel narrowed and a bend shut out the daylight. Lighting matches with one hand as he trailed his rifle with the other, each moment expecting the enraged beast to charge out of the darkness, Giles crawled ahead for fifty feet—the longest and slowest he had ever traveled. Then he came to another bend. He lighted another match and peered around it.

The bear was stretched out, dead. Giles almost collapsed. For several minutes he could not even scratch another match. He just sat there and sweated.

The worst of all the killers that exacted bloody toll from herds and flocks was the gray or Great Plains wolf, called the buffalo wolf or loafer wolf on the prairies and the lobo wolf in the Southwest—a near but larger relative of the Eastern timber wolf which was the subject of an earlier chapter. No animal has ever been more hated. But the early stockmen who cursed it also respected and admired it. It was big and husky—as much as 175 pounds of bones and muscle. Its eyes were as sharp as its teeth, which have been known to crunch through a two-inch-thick club with a single bite. It had keen ears and a highly sensitive nose. It was fierce and deadly when it had to fight, but it also had an uncanny ability to avoid its human foes and all their devices for its destruction.

Big packs of the gray killers hung around the flanks and rear of browsing herds of buffalo, their natural prey. They pulled down and devoured calves and weak older animals, and even ganged up on pugnacious young bulls when hunger drove them to it. Although they quickly acquired a taste for beef and mutton, they did not concentrate on cattle until the buffalo were gone. They then split up into smaller packs and attacked the widely scattered bands of cattle and sheep, finding it much easier meat to get than the sturdy buffalo had ever been.

In the early days in the West, wolves had little fear of men, but when they started to kill cattle, the stockmen's Sharps and Winchesters taught them to be wary; even in the worst-infested districts they were seldom seen by daylight. The cattlemen turned to strychnine as their best weapon against the wolf. Many outfits hired old-time wolvers who had made a business of poisoning wolves for their pelts. The cowhands were taught by these experts, and it became a part of the unwritten code of the range that no one should ever pass a carcass without slipping a big shot of strychnine into it in the hope of killing a wolf. But the smarter wolves soon realized that eating carrion was likely to be bad for their health, so they went in for fresh kills every time they wanted a meal. In some districts they killed half the year's calf crop!

Next the stockmen tried dogs. Massingale, a professional hunter in the Little Missouri country in the eighteen eighties, had a pack of greyhounds and big crossbreds which killed an average of two hundred wolves a year. Stockmen of the Sun River district in Montana imported a pack of greyhounds and staghounds which accounted for 146 wolves in a single season. In open country such dogs were faster than a wolf, but when the going was rough they were useless because of the wolf's greater stamina.

Hunters teamed up in jeep-and-plane combinations with two-way radio direction to outwit the elusive coyote. This practice is now no longer legal.

That stamina seemed almost boundless. There was a big timber wolf in the eighteen nineties, for example, that had been killing deer on Grand Island, a game preserve in Lake Superior. Several expert hunters followed its tracks in the snow for four days before one of them got in a shot and wounded it. After that they worked in relays, trailing the animal—by lantern at night—almost around the clock. It took them two weeks to kill it.

Perhaps the most successful wolf hunter who depended on the rifle was Bill Cozzens, of Idaho, who did his hunting on skis and was among the first to sign up as a government hunter. After each snowfall he scouted the country for wolf tracks; when he found one he slipped on white cap and clothing. Then, effectively camouflaged and moving faster on his skis than the wolf could run in the fresh snow, he stalked it until he got close enough to shoot.

Many thousands of wolves were killed by poisoning, hounding, and shooting, but the survivors were fast breeders and their numbers increased; the yearly wolf litter averages seven whelps.

The man who found the right answer to the West's predator problem never traveled beyond the Mississippi. He was Sewell Newhouse, the first manufacturer of efficient steel traps. Born in 1806, Newhouse grew up in Oneida County, New York. He made his first traps when he was seventeen, using old ax blades for material; for the next two decades he made about two thousand traps a year by hand. They were used all over the eastern United States and in Canada.

Newhouse became a member of the Oneida Community—an experiment in cooperative industry—which in 1855 took over the manufacture of his traps, providing him with a workshop and helpers. In the next dozen years Newhouse and his assistants devised power machines to make all the trap parts. Increased production lowered costs and prices,

and by the middle of the eighteen sixties he was making traps in eight sizes, to catch anything from a mouse to a grizzly, at the rate of a hundred thousand a year. By 1890 the Newhouse trap was as much a wilderness stand-by as the Winchester rifle.

Sizable bounties made wolf-trapping profitable, and men finally learned the one weak spot in the wolf's armor against its human enemies—the doglike regularity of its habits, which made it particularly susceptible to trapping. Nearly all wolves have circular hunting routes, which they travel on schedule. At intervals along these runways they have "scent posts" that they can no more pass without visiting than a city dog can skip a fire hydrant. The trapper who can locate these posts and predict when the wolf will visit them, can set his traps with considerable assurance that he will catch a wolf.

Several years of systematic effort by government hunters working in cooperation with stockmen's associations and state agencies—which more than matched each federal dollar spent for predator extermination, not only brought the gray wolf under control but virtually eliminated all wolves in the lower forty-eight states. In fact, some conservationists, alarmed at the impending extinction of some wolf species, have instigated restocking nucleus wolf packs in certain areas of the U.S. However, these experimental stocking programs have so far proven mostly unsuccessful. This is due in large measure to the complex social order of a wolf pack. Many experts feel that in order for wolves to be successfully relocated it will be necessary to trap an entire pack and move all members to the new home. Such a trapping operation would be extremely difficult if not altogether impossible.

Ironically, the salvation of the wolf may prove to be his newly gained status as a desirable game animal. British Columbia now charges non-residents seventy-five dollars for a license to bag a single wolf. When a game animal proves to be a valuable revenue-producing natural resource, government agencies are more inclined to take steps which will insure its continued well being.

This factor has been largely responsible for the remarkable comeback of the mountain lion in recent years. In some western states where the timid cats were once relentlessly pursued by bounty hunters, they are now sought only by hunters who pay guides as much as five hundred dollars to find and "tree" a trophy lion. One far western state recently made quite a big to-do over the fact that their game biologists had successfully stocked mountain lions into an area from which they had been eliminated earlier in this century. This action points up a complete reversal of popular attitude toward the graceful predator which prevailed only a few decades ago.

The status of the wily coyote is still very much in question. In 1973 the Federal Government issued a ban on coyote poisoning and trapping on all federal lands. Western sheep and cattle growers who lease grazing rights on these lands reported a sharp increase in coyote-caused livestock losses within months after the ban went into effect. Ranchers also report being frustrated in attempts to control coyote populations even on their own lands by an Environmental Protection Agency restriction on the interstate shipment of poisons. Emotions on both sides of the coyote control debate run high and it may yet be some time before a compromise is found. At present though there is no doubt that brer coyote is flourishing and finding life easier than in past generations.

CHAPTER 15

Hunting Yesterday and Today

The founding fathers who signed the Declaration of Independence would have been perplexed and then astounded if they could have peered into a crystal ball and viewed the two hundred year saga of America's wildlife. They might not have been too surprised at the excesses which brought about the decimation of the continent's vast buffalo herds or the extinction of the passenger pigeon or marsh hen. Colonial settlers viewed their wildlife as a resource to be exploited whenever and wherever possible. There was also a generally accepted attitude that while the availability of game played an important part of the settling of the wilderness to the West it would disappear as land was cleared and farms cultivated. But by then game would not be so important to survival and not necessarily missed. The prevailing attitude toward wildlife was that it was to be sacrificed to the young nation's growth—that this was a natural factor in human progress and that no power could prevent it. This attitude no doubt hastened the elimination of wildlife in many areas because it led hunters to believe that the game was doomed anyway and if they didn't shoot and trap the remaining herds or flocks someone else would.

Even the slaughter of the buffalo may have seemed an inevitable part of America's "manifest destiny" but the crystal ball gazers would undoubtedly have been amazed at the deadly efficiency of the American hunting rifle of the late 1800's and the men who used them.

But the most astounding thing they would have seen—by far—would be the success of the wildlife conservation programs begun in the early decades of the twentieth century. The concept of civilized man living within an ongoing relationship with nearby game species was almost totally alien to their personal experience as well as the lessons of past history. In Europe, for example, the only surviving game was totally controlled by the noble classes and jealously protected from the common folk. It was assumed, no doubt correctly, that if the masses had access to the game herds, hunting would not survive for long. When the democratic principles of the United States were established it was doubtlessly assumed by our more aristocratic forefathers that in time the country's game would inevitably perish due to the fact that it was free to any farmer, clerk or laborer who owned or could borrow a firearm. But this it was certainly also assumed, must be the price of a free democracy. This is why our current game management practices—which are founded almost entirely on a willingness to co-operate and work toward a common goal, by twenty million sportsmen—would probably have been unthinkable two centuries ago.

Despite the best intentions of game-conservation minded sportsmen early attempts at wildlife preservation and perpetuation often proved disappointing and sometimes even disastrous. By the time of the First World War there were serious attempts underway to protect America's dwindling wildlife population but there were still bitter lessons to be learned. The most important lesson was that game, or any other wildlife, cannot be stockpiled and that overprotection can be as bad, and sometimes worse, than no protection at all. This is a fundamental fact in sound management.

An example of well-intentioned game

management that almost turned sour is the saga of the Pennsylvania whitetail deer. By the turn of this century the Keystone state's whitetail population had all but been eliminated. In earlier years that state's sportsmen had enjoyed a bountiful supply of deer, turkey, bear and upland birds but constant pressure from market hunters, plus extensive farming and lumbering operations had reduced the game population to a critical level. European immigrants, in particular, who flocked to Pennsylvania during the last half of the 19th century to toil in the state's coal fields, were especially keen on hunting, a sport which had been denied them in their native homelands, and in a few short years succeeded in proving that the game protection practices of the European landholders were well justified.

In 1896 a Board of Game Commissioners was appointed to do something about the poor hunting situation but they were supplied

The buck laws were so effective at times that crops were damaged by over-population of deer. However many hunters were so indoctrinated that when doe seasons were opened, they protested.

with very little to work with. The first funding allowed only four hundred dollars *per year!* Nonetheless it was a start. In 1913 hunters were required to buy a one dollar hunting license. With this money to work with the Pennsylvania Game Commission, guided by such visionary sportsmen as John M. Phillips, established game refuges on state owned lands. In 1906 fifty whitetail deer, which had been trapped in Michigan, were released on the newly established refuges.

But with the restocking of the deer, the Commission's troubles were just beginning. The refuge plan was not a popular one. Many meat hunters could not—or would not—understand the reasoning behind using their license dollars to stock deer and then putting the animals in areas where no hunting was allowed. Accordingly they went hunting anyway and ran head on into a new denizen of the forest—the game warden. These early confrontations were sometimes bloody and it was not until the passage of stricter laws governing hunting and gun ownership among aliens that peace was once more established.

In 1907 Pennsylvania passed a "buck only" law which prohibited the taking of does during hunting season. The purpose of this law of course was to protect the breeding stock and thus insure maximum growth of the herds. The "buck only" law was a smart idea at the time, but was, in time, to result in a near catastrophe.

The "buck only" law, combined with Pennsylvania's ideal game habitat caused a remarkably rapid rise in the deer population. Sportsmen, overjoyed to see herds of plump deer in areas where before there had been none, became enthusiastic supporters of the concept of bagging only bucks. But in less than two decades the deer herds had increased to the point that they were literally eating themselves out of feeding grounds. In 1923 the overflowing deer herds were raiding farms and gardens and causing so much crop

damage that the Commission had to seek ways to reduce their numbers.

The obvious answer was a special doe season, which would not only reduce the herd but bring its reproducing capacity back in line with the carrying capacity of the deer lands. But alas, the "buck only" campaign had been *too* effective and now sportsmen balked at the idea of lining up their sights on a female animal. Diehard buck-law men paraded through towns in deer country carrying placards reading, "Don't be yellow and kill a doe!" But by 1928 the deer had become so obviously overpopulated that the Commission had to enact a hunt for antlerless deer *only!* By then many sportsmen could see for themselves what was about to happen if the herd wasn't reduced and despite loud protest from some of their fellow hunters, turned out in sufficient number to crop the herd by some seventy thousand does. Ten years later an antlerless deer hunt was held which resulted in a bag of 171,000 females. Two years later a mixed-sex hunt had a total kill of 186,575 deer, proof enough for even the most determined "buck only" holdout that the earlier doe hunts had not harmed the quality of Pennsylvania's deer hunting but only enhanced it.

In the year of the nation's Bicentennial, Pennsylvania's 1.3 million hunters will pay out approximately nine million dollars in hunting licenses and fees and bag over 100,000 whitetail, a far cry from an earlier day when the state's Game Department had only four hundred dollars to spend in a year and the big game was said to be "shot out."

The story of Arizona's Kaibab deer didn't have such a happy ending. Unlike Pennsylvania, which had virtually no deer at the turn of the century, the breathtakingly scenic Kaibab plateau on the northern rim of the Grand Canyon had a healthy mule deer population. It was an isolated region, to be sure, but hearty hunters who packed into the wilderness bagged some of the greatest trophy deer to be found anywhere. In 1906, however, by presidential decree, the Kaibab was made the "Grand Canyon Game Preserve" and all hunting was thenceforth outlawed. Also, just to make sure the deer thrived in carefree contentment, an energetic program was inaugurated to rid the area of all predators. During the next quarter century thirty wolves were killed (bringing them to extinction in that area), 4,889 coyotes, 554 bobcats, 781 mountain lions and an unknown number of eagles were exterminated by government-paid wardens.

Also, at the same time the privately owned herds of cattle and sheep which grazed the area were on the increase. Likewise, the "protected" deer were rapidly increasing their numbers. In 1906, when the preserve was created, there were an estimated 4,000 deer in the area, thereafter the population increased by about twenty per cent per year; 4800, 5760, 6912, 8294, etc. By the early 1920s the population had grown to approximately 100,000 and as many as *seventeen hundred* head could be seen grazing in one meadow, according to eyewitnesses. Back in 1918 the Forest Supervisor had reported that there were too many deer on the Kaibab but at that time too much of a good thing was a strange problem to reckon with. So nothing was done.

The end came in the winter of 1924–25. The deer died by the thousands and those strong enough to stand stripped the area of every leaf, twig and blade of grass. It was as if a swarm of locusts had invaded the landscape. That year hunting had again been allowed on the Kaibab and predator control had been halted the year before, but it was too little too late. Within five years four out of every five deer on the Kaibab died of starvation or diseases related to an insufficient diet.

The Kaibab deer population is once again healthy and, due to sound game management

practices, producing trophies. Nonetheless it stands as a classic example of the fallacy of "stockpiling" game.

In the country as a whole, there were about four hundred thousand fewer whitetails in 1959 than there were ten years before, according to estimates compiled by the U.S. Fish and Wildlife Service. But hunting in 1959 was as good as—and in many states better than—it was in 1949. The decreases in deer populations came in states which retained the buck law too long, and in consequence had to reduce their herds drastically to fit them to the available food supply. Wisconsin's adherence to the buck law until 1941 resulted in over-browsing, which ruined most of the north-country wintering yards, and in statewide depletion. To save the whitetails from threatened starvation an "any-deer" season was opened. Nearly half of the 123,000 deer killed were antlerless. Some sportsmen thought that the whitetails had been shot down so close to extinction that there never would be good deer hunting in Wisconsin again. They were mistaken. Only three years later two hundred thousand hunters set an all-time record by killing fifty-five thousand bucks. Michigan kept the buck law until forty thousand of its deer, which could have been harvested by an either-sex season, starved to death during a hard winter in the mid-forties.

Maine, which never had a buck law and always offers good deer hunting, has twice as many whitetails as it had twenty years ago, yet it had average kills of forty thousand from 1956 to 1958. New York had trouble with uneven hunter distribution—too few in the Adirondack back country, too many almost everywhere else. But in 1958 there was a kill of forty-two thousand bucks and—in a one-day, any-deer season—twenty-four thousand antlerless deer. West Virginia has allowed, in recent years, either-sex hunting in areas where deer are plentiful and bucks-only hunting where they are not. The normal hunters' take is about eighteen thousand. North of the Canadian line, whitetails are almost unbeliev-ably plentiful in some parts of both New Brunswick and Nova Scotia.

Southern deer hunting varies from fair to excellent. In mountain areas, most of which were almost shot out fifty years ago, the whitetails have made a remarkable comeback, as a result of restocking on game-management areas in national forests and on state-owned lands. Around 1900 the last deer was killed in the mountains of northern Georgia. Said the man who shot it: "Mortalgod, there jest weren't no sense in leavin' that pore ol' buck lonesome in this-hyer big country." Now

Georgia has thirty-five thousand whitetails. North Carolina has three times as many deer as it had twenty years ago. Virginia, with a herd of 150,000, has ten times as many. Arkansas' whitetails have increased from 9,000 to 110,000, Missouri's from 700 to 200,000!

In the Northern and Western states, an early game-conservation measure was the banning of the use of dogs in deer hunting, but "hounding" whitetails is still lawful in much of the South. In the coastal swamps from Virginia to Georgia, where deer are and always have been plentiful, it is the most pop-

The almost universal use of the automobile revolutionized hunting. Men could drive to deer country one evening, hunt the next day, and drive home that night, often with a whitetail roped to the fender.

ular and in some areas the only practical way to hunt them.

During the thirty or more years it took to build up today's huge herds, there were drastic changes in deer-hunting conditions, and consequently in deer-hunting methods, all over the country. The fundamental cause was the automobile, which could carry hunters over new roads to good hunting country; a tremendous increase in the number of hunters; and the even greater increase in the number of deer. At the end of World War I, there was a thirty per cent increase in the number of hunters—to more than three million in 1919, then to more than four million in 1926, and to nearly seven million in 1930.

The results of the new conditions were first apparent in the whitetail areas of the East and Lakes states. Before World War I a deer hunt meant, for most hunters, a week or more of back-country camping and long days of still hunting or trailing (preferably with a powdering of snow on the ground that made it possible for the hunter to pick up the tracks of a big buck) in vast reaches of woods and brush in which one seldom crossed a road or saw another hunter.

The almost universal use of the automobile changed all that. Now there are comparatively few permanent camps in deer country; most hunters who stay overnight sleep in trailers or nearby motels. There are many short-order Nimrods—men who drive up to the deer country one evening, hunt the next day, and drive home that night, often with a whitetail roped to the fender. Most of these hurried hunters never go as far as half a mile into the brush. Instead, they line the roads hoping for shots, with the result that one-tenth of the deer, most of them does or young bucks, are subjected to nine-tenths of the hunting pressure. Many an old buck with a trophy rack of horns who is smart enough to stay in the back country goes through the season without even being seen. With the woods cut up into sections by roads picketed by standers, trailing and stillhunting have become unrewarding except in a few remote areas. A hunter does not like to chase a deer out of the brush for a road hunter to shoot. Drives—productive since colonial days—have again become the most common method of hunting. It often pays off just to pick a likely spot and sit there until a deer wanders or is driven within shooting distance. Some of the biggest whitetails are killed on farms. Old-timers complain that deer hunting isn't the sport it used to be. They're right, but it grows more popular each year.

In the West, the deer population has been growing even more rapidly than in the East. State game commission estimates indicate that twenty years ago there were a million more deer east of the Mississippi than there were west of it. Now there are a quarter of a million more mule deer, blacktails, and whitetails west of the river than there are whitetails east of it. The West has about two and a half times more mule deer and whitetails than it had in 1937, and four times as many blacktails.

The principle reasons for this impressive increase have been: intelligent management by the state game commissions, most of which used the buck law to rebuild their depleted herds but switched to controlled either-sex hunting in time to keep the animals fairly well in balance with their food supply; effective protection against illegal hunting by state and federal authorities; and increased growth of good browse in areas where there has been extensive timber-cutting.

California, Oregon, and Washington have magnificent herds of blacktails in their coastal regions and mule deer inland. The other Western states have big populations of mule deer; Colorado, Utah, and Nevada probably have too many for the good of their range. Most of the Western whitetails are in Texas, but several other states have enough for good hunting.

Deer-hunting conditions and methods vary widely over the vast expanse of the West, but in general they have changed less than in the East and South. The national forests and public-domain lands offer the hunter great roadless areas as primitive as they were at the turn of the century. Almost everyone uses a car to get to good deer territory, but there are far fewer road hunters than in the East. In big open country horses are used for hunting, but not nearly so much as they used to be. Guides and dude ranches keep them for their patrons, but in today's West probably five hundred sportsmen do their hunting afoot to one who does it in the saddle. Deer hunting is excellent almost everywhere in the West, and the average yearly kill of about three-quarters of a million is three times that of the East.

Plentiful annual crops of "dividend" deer which may be harvested by hunters without decreasing the breeding stock on which future sport depends are the backbone of American big-game hunting. We have such crops now, and there is good reason for confidence that we will always have them.

The future of elk hunting also seems to be assured. The lordly wapiti now is found al-

Expensive pack-trail travel has become necessary to hunt elk, which has gradually retreated to high, rough country.

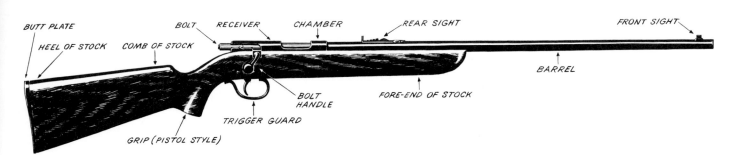

BUTT PLATE BOLT RECEIVER CHAMBER REAR SIGHT FRONT SIGHT
HEEL OF STOCK COMB OF STOCK BARREL
BOLT HANDLE FORE-END OF STOCK
TRIGGER GUARD
GRIP (PISTOL STYLE)

The most universally used hunting rifle today has a bolt action, which is strong, simple and easy to take apart.

most exclusively in rough, high country which calls for expensive pack-trail travel, so hunting pressure is not nearly so heavy as it is on deer. Elk have a lower breeding potential than deer because they mature at an older age, but they have also increased in number—by at least fifty per cent in the past decade.

There were once native elk in Pennsylvania, but the last one was killed shortly after the Civil War. Fifty years later, some Western elk were stocked in Cameron County, and a hundred were killed in open seasons between 1923 and 1931. A few of their progeny survive; during most deer seasons one or two are killed by myopic hunters who mistake them for whitetails, or claim they have done so. There are also some descendants of stocked elk in the mountains of southwest Virginia; several were killed in a short open season in 1958. But the wapiti's crop-raiding proclivities make it an undesirable game animal in thickly settled country, and there is no chance of, or reason for, its restoration in the East.

In the early nineteen twenties the Western antelope seemed doomed to extinction, but the establishment of federal refuges and the careful nursing by state game commissions of the remnants of native herds saved the pronghorns. Big game such as elk and pronghorn are not only more abundant than just a few years ago but can now be hunted in areas where they didn't even previously exist. A shining example of this is New Mexico's Mescalero Apache Indian Reservation which now offers outstanding trophy elk as well as deer, bear and turkey. Wise game management has made this possible. Not only are hunters treated to fine shooting but the hunting permits sold by the reservation represent a substantial cash income. Everyone benefits.

In time some states will even offer big game species that were unknown on this continent when the pilgrims came. The ringneck pheasant, chukar and Hungarian partridge are outstanding examples of "exotic" game birds which were foreigners to these shores a century ago but have since become part of our hunting heritage. But even bigger things are in store. New Mexico, for example, is offering limited hunting for a beautiful African antelope called the oryx and Texas has a season on the odd-looking aoudad. These and other species have been hunted on private shooting preserves, most notably in Texas, for some years now but the day is approaching when they will be hunted on public lands.

Despite the success record of America's modern day conservation programs some laws are occasionally passed without proper analysis of the consequences. An example of this is the Wild Horse and Burro Act. This law was passed amid a series of high pressure arguments which were long on emotion but short on forethought. The original purpose was certainly sound—the prevention of cruelty to the small bands of wild horses and burros which are found in some parts of the Western states. Actually these are not true wild animals but only the offspring of domestic animals which had "gone wild." Before the passage of the Wild Horse and Burro Act they were killed—sometimes cruelly—for hides and pet food.

Now protected, the burros in particular have proven heartier than most wildlife and highly aggressive, driving deer, desert sheep and other wildlife from life giving water holes. Consequently some wildlife species are having a difficult time surviving in desert areas. If the Federal Act is not amended soon to allow for control of the aggressive burros, deer and sheep may become extinct in some regions.

The "balance of nature" is a popular but chronically misused phrase. Preservationists (those who want to retain wildlife in a pristine, undisturbed state), speak romantically of the days in our nation's past history when the early settlers, and the red man before that, lived in blissful harmony with the creatures about him and "all nature was in balance." Actually we are living in a time when nature is on a more even keel than ever before. Two hundred years ago and before, nature was not neat and orderly with just the right numbers of game and predators mixed with the correct proportions of natural food and cover. The closest thing to a "balance" was actually a cycle which occurred over several years.

A deer "cycle," for example, could begin with a devastating forest fire which could have resulted from natural causes such as lightning. Immediately after the fire there would be no wildlife in the region, but soon green shoots would spring through the blackened earth. Deer are particularly fond of low lying browse and as young trees sprouted the deer population would rapidly increase. In time though the trees would be too tall for the deer to browse on and their higher branches would form a leafy canopy over the forest floor, shielding the sun and preventing further plant growth.

By now predators would have moved into the area and the deer population would fall off to the bare carrying capacity of the range. If the predators failed in their task other, more insidious predators such as body parasites, and diseases would take their toll. Sometimes

The lever-action repeater (top) is operated by flicking the lever forward and back, allowing the shooter to reload without taking the rifle from his shoulder. The slide-action repeater (center), which reloads when the slide is pulled back and pushed forward again, is a very fast action in the hands of a trained shooter. The autoloading repeater, or semiautomatic (bottom), which reloads itself after each shot, is fine for a safe shooter, but not for the inexperienced.

a mass die-off would occur which would all but strip the forest of deer until another fire came and the cycle began again. This was the "balance" of nature.

Today's wildlife managers can measure and predict the needs of our wildlife with remarkable accuracy. The carrying capacity of any given deer range, be it in Pennsylvania, Michigan or Arizona, can be determined by calculating the population and reproduction rate of the inhabitant deer and a very accurate prediction of the number of adult deer that must be removed can be made. Sport hunters then harvest the surplus.

Thus the hunter is not only a tool in the management of our wildlife resources but has actually become a vital element in the modern balance of nature. Whether he hunts elk or only cottontail rabbits his hunting license dollars benefit non-game species as well. This is because it is impossible to improve the habitat of hunted game animals without also improving conditions for all other wildlife, from songbirds to field mice.

The sportsmen's willingness to contribute money to the well being of wildlife stands without equal in any field of endeavor or philanthropy. In one area of contribution alone, a self-imposed tax on sporting guns and ammunition, sportsmen will contribute approximately $58,000,000 in the year of the nation's 200th birthday. Another $12,000 will be contributed in the form of Duck stamps, another self-imposed assessment. Many more millions will be paid out of pocket by sportsmen to support hundreds of other local and state programs. Ducks Unlimited, a hunter-financed, non-governmental organization, has spent millions of dollars in past years buying northern wetlands so that future generations of Americans—hunters and non-hunters alike —will be assured the thrill of seeing huge flocks of ducks and geese making their annual migration. Far more threatening to the survival of waterfowl than any hunter is the con-

tinued drainage of the northern nesting grounds. The funds raised by Ducks Unlimited have guaranteed that there will be a place not only for ducks to build their nests in coming years but also non-hunted swans and rare water birds.

A remarkable phenomenon of modern hunting is the return, by many sportsmen, to muzzle loading rifles such as those used in Colonial days. Perhaps it is appropriate on our nation's Bicentennial to try hunting with the arms used by the colonists but black powder shooting is more than just a novelty or passing craze. Some states have special big game seasons for muzzle loaders only and some shooters have found hunting with the long rifles so enjoyable that they've given up modern cartridge rifles and shotguns altogether. Much of the charm no doubt lies in the grace and beauty of the "Kentucky" long rifle itself. In an age of mass produced gadgetry the long rifle stands as a symbol of an age of great gun craftsmanship when beauty as well as function was considered a necessary element of a fine sporting arm.

This doesn't mean that modern technology has been foresworn altogether. Today's muzzle loaders, although close look-alikes of the early flintlock or percussion rifles, utilize better steels and precision rifling techniques which produce a degree of accuracy unknown with most of the original firearms.

Arms development in America has taken some surprising turns over the past two hundred years. Around the time of the Civil War and for several years thereafter the main thrust in gun development was toward increased firepower. The lever action, the pump and finally, the fully automatic machine gun were all results of what was considered to be a need for increased firepower. Yet, today's sportsmen tend to place relatively little emphasis on the ability to produce a hail of bullets. Lever action rifles such as Winchester's Model 1894 (which has sold in the mil-

Annual bird restocking has become common in many states. Special compartmented boxes are set out in a field to allow the birds, such as the ringneck pheasants above, to free themselves.

lions), continue to be popular but the average big game hunter is more concerned with accuracy and cartridge performance so the bolt action has become the standard American hunting rifle.

Since the Second World War there have been advances in rifle performance—especially accuracy—which would have amazed the founding fathers. Rifles and sights that make it possible to hit a deer or an elk, or even a woodchuck at several hundred yards are commonplace. A new type of target shooter, the bench rester, who fires from a solid rest and is more concerned about firing a tight five or ten shot group than just hitting a bullseye, uses rifles so accurate that the shots frequently form only one small hole scarcely larger than that made by a single bullet!

The trend in tomorrow's rifles will undoubtedly be toward even greater accuracy. Today's hunters, popular legend to the con-

trary, are more skilled as marksmen than our fathers and grandfathers and they demand rifles equal to their skill. This factor has contributed to the super long range class of cartridges popularly known as the Magnum. Such rounds as the 7mm Remington Magnum, .300 Weatherby Magnum and .300 Winchester Magnum feature remarkably flat trajectories which make possible well placed and deadly hits on deer-sized game out to four hundred yards.

A very interesting trend in American gun making is the continued emphasis on high quality and reliability. And the same Yankee ingenuity that first produced interchangeability of gun parts and mass production has managed to combine mass production with the look and feel of fine handcraftsmanship. There is no doubt that many guns are purchased by individuals who simply appreciate owning a fine piece of craftsmanship.

This is especially true of shotgunners. Despite the availability of self-feeding shotguns which fire and function at the pull of a trigger, there is an increasing demand for high quality over-and-under and side-by-side shotguns. The spiraling cost of ultra-skilled hand labor has caused the price of some of the finest shotguns to be as much as ten thousand dollars or even more, yet the demand exceeds the supply more than ever before.

A service that will undoubtedly make tremendous contribution to the quality of tomorrow's hunting is the hunter safety programs now being offered by local sportsmen's clubs in conjunction with state conservation agencies and the National Rifle Association. These programs not only train youngsters in marksmanship and safe gun handling but also instill in them a respect for wildlife and other people's property. This means that the "slob" hunter—the fellow who shoots signs, tears down fences and damages property—just may become an "extinct" species someday. With this kind of hunter out of the picture, landowners will be more willing to allow responsible sportsmen to harvest game on their property. In fact this is already happening. Most notably are the large land-holding lumber and paper companies who are not only permitting hunters access to their lands, but are actually hiring wildlife management and planning professionals to help bring about safe, effective hunting and a good balance of game. These are examples of active programs that will insure good hunting across the land for many years to come.

INDEX

THE INDIANS

1820

1600s

1700s

1850